Mira Silverstein's
GUIDE TO
COMBINATION STITCHES

Mira Silverstein's

GUIDE TO COMBINATION STITCHES

XXXXXXXXXXXXXXXXXXXXXXXXXXXXXXXXXXXXXXXXXXXXXXXXXXX

Exciting Needlework Projects, Patterns, and Designs Anyone Can Make

ARTWORK BY ROBERTA FRAUWIRTH

PHOTOGRAPHY BY SANDY L. STUDIOS

DAVID McKAY COMPANY, INC.
New York

I wish to take this opportunity to thank all those who worked with me in a professional capacity and especially Barbara Anderson who helped edit this book.

Cover needlework designed and worked by Cheryl Ruehle, courtesy Paternayan Brothers. Log Cabin Patchwork (pages 72–77) designed and worked by Diane Musten, courtesy Paternayan Brothers. (Both the cover and Log Cabin Patchwork needlework were prizewinners in the 1976 Paternayan Needlework Competition.) Bicycle Seat Cover (page 82) copyright © 1977 Downe Publishing, Inc. Reprinted by permission of Ladies' Home Journal Needle & Craft. Designed by Elise Silverstein. Envelope Handbag (pages 54-56) designed by Huquette Braverman. Victor's Pillow (page 53) designed and worked by Harriet Alonso. Small Stylized Birds (pages 64–66) designed and worked by Helen Maris. Partridge in a Tree (page 62) designed and worked by Roberta Frauwirth.

Samples finished by Ida Gold, Harriet Alonso, Carol B. Kempner, Mindi Kantor, Shirley Kantor, Elise Silverstein, Gigi Strauss, Joan Hyman, Mary McGregor, Eve Charny, Marie Gunther, and Jane Benson.

Diagrams on pages 18, 79, 115, 116, and 118 by Shirley Rose.

Library of Congress Cataloging in Publication Data

Silverstein, Mira.
   Mira Silverstein's Guide to combination stitches.

   1. Canvas embroidery.   I. Title.   II. Title: Guide to combination stitches.
TT778.C3S542   1977   746.4'4   77-10919
ISBN 0-679-50820-1
ISBN 0-679-50786-8 pbk.

10 9 8 7 6 5 4 3 2 1

Manufactured in the United States of America

Designed by Jacques Chazaud

For Elise

XX

CONTENTS

XX

INTRODUCTION

Needlework is the general term used to describe all work done with the threaded needle, both by hand and by machine. It is divided into two main categories: utilitarian needlework or sewing, where stitches perform the basic function of joining fabrics; and decorative needlework, where stitches are used to create a design which decorates the fabric surface and becomes part of the fabric itself.

There are various kinds of decorative needlework. The most familiar are listed below.

Embroidery is a term most often used to describe decorative needlework applied to fine, densely woven fabrics, such as linen, silk, or cotton.

Crewel is embroidery worked with wool yarn or yarns of similar texture on compatible fabrics, such as linen or wool.

Canvas work refers to the kind of fabric used and not a special kind of needlework. Canvas is an open-mesh, even-weave fabric and the stitches worked on it will be a little more "patterned," or uniform, than those worked on denser cloth.

Counted-thread indicates the manner of workmanship when the design is not painted on the fabric but is reproduced from a graphed outline. The graph is counted in stitches or stitch units, and the fabric is counted in threads. The more threads alloted to a stitch unit, the larger the gauge of the design.

Surface embroidery is a figure of speech since all embroidery is worked on the surface.

Needlepoint is sometimes used to describe canvas work in general and the Half-cross or Continental stitch in particular. However, it is not a stitch. It is only another term for work with a threaded needle, or "point of the needle."

Creative stitchery refers to the most artistic form of needlework when the stitches are used to create an original design on the fabric rather than first painting the design on the fabric and then

1

filling it in with stitches. Creative stitchery is also a general term for embroidery or stitchery. It is the art or craft of decorating fabric with lines and loops in interesting patterns with the aid of a threaded needle. The lines and loops are known as stitches.

The basic, or line stitch is a straight line between two points and is executed with a threaded needle. The threaded needle is brought to the surface of the fabric, carried across it in a predetermined direction, then brought back to the reverse side of the fabric to complete the stitch.

The line stitch may be long or short, horizontal or vertical, or slanted to any degree; but in itself it is only a line. Worked end to end, the line stitch will, in some cases, form a curvilinear outline. However, it cannot curve or flex by itself without being anchored in some way by another stitch, in which case the line stitch is altered before completion. All knotted, looped, chained, and tied stitches are based on this manipulation.

When a number of line stitches are worked side by side, crossed over, or placed in any combination to form a specific pattern, they create what is called a stitch formation, or stitch pattern.

Each stitch formation has its own distinctive texture when worked over a large area. This texture is immediately altered with the slightest adjustment in the length and number of lines in the individual stitch pattern.

There are hundreds of stitch patterns in the lexicon of needlework. They are often identified by name and place of origin. Most of them are minor variations of a handful of classic patterns.

This is a beginners' introduction to basic decorative needlework. The accent is on the construction of stitches and stitch patterns that, once mastered, will enable the beginner to create a wide variety of beautiful and useful projects. Each stitch and stitch pattern will be outlined in step-by-step detail, and its special properties and usage will be explained. Many design projects are introduced in this book. However, beginners are encouraged to further diversify and explore, to invent new stitch patterns, to create unusual color combinations, and to alter, adapt, or adjust. The possibilities are endless.

XX

IMPORTANT
INFORMATION

Threading the Needle and Anchoring Yarn

For those who have never worked with canvas and yarn, a little practice is recommended before embarking on a large project. The best way to learn anything is by doing.

Read the sections on materials and supplies and buy a small piece of firm, interlocked # 12 canvas, a few small skeins of Persian-type yarn in assorted colors, and a blunt-pointed needle.

Cut the canvas into small easy-to-handle pieces, and cover the edge with paper or plastic tape. (Surgical and cellophane tapes will not adhere properly to canvas.) Even if the canvas does not ravel, the edges are rough and should be taped.

To thread the needle, fold the end of a strand of yarn over the needle and hold both firmly between thumb and forefinger. Pull the needle away without disturbing the yarn fold. Press the fold between the fingers until yarn is flat and barely visible. Press the eye of the tapestry needle over this fold and don't release the yarn until the needle is threaded.

To begin work on a bare canvas, pull the threaded needle up through the fabric, leaving a tail of about 2″ on the reverse side. Hold this tail down with one hand while you work the first few stitches over it, catching some of the yarn in the process.

Subsequent strands should be slipped through a worked area and held in place for the first stitch or two. Don't use knots in canvas work—they can almost always be detected. If a knot becomes undone, there probably won't be enough yarn to reanchor it, and several stitches may have to be taken out and replaced.

To end off the yarn, slide it into a worked area and keep all visible tails clipped. Tails will tangle the working yarn and the wool will shed a fuzz which will carry onto the right side of the work and become imbedded in the stitches.

How to Read and Interpret Diagrams and Graph Outlines

The designs in this book are shown in diagrams or graphs. A *diagram* is the outline or framework of a needlepoint design. A diagram is shown complete on one page or in sections on two or more pages. Yarn colors are outlined within the diagram and indicated by numbers.

To transfer a diagram to canvas, it must first be reproduced on another sheet of paper as is, or enlarged if necessary. The canvas is then placed over this paper, and the design is traced with a fine-point indelible ink pen.

A diagram may be altered and the stitches changed to suit the individual needleworker. Parts and pieces from one diagram may be combined with those of another to create any number of design variations.

A *graph* is a skeletal construction of a design. It indicates not only the design outline but also each and every stitch within it. The colors are indicated with symbols such as half-crosses and crosses, lines, dots, etc. The code is shown in the corner of the page.

A graph is also called a counted-stitch pattern because it is reproduced stitch-for-stitch and not within a drawn outline. This is the most accurate way to reproduce a needlepoint design, but it leaves little room for creative alterations.

To reproduce a counted-stitch pattern, divide the canvas into a number of equal squares. Draw the lines over the canvas threads with fine-point acrylic pen. Although the stitches are painted inside the graph squares, they are worked *over* the canvas threads or meshes, and this is the way they should be translated.

Graph paper is generally divided into small squares of ten or more to the inch. The square inch is outlined with a heavier line, which makes the counting of stitches much simpler.

By turning your canvas into a graph (Figure 1), the stitch-by-stitch count becomes less formidable.

FIGURE 1
Creating a grid to facilitate counted thread stitchery

Begin at any point, and work the groups of stitches in consecutive order. Do not skip from one area to another. Complete the entire design before doing the background. If a graph design seems too complicated, color in the coded stitch outlines. Use transparent colors that are bright enough to show color placement without covering the code marks. To enlarge a graph pattern, use a canvas with a larger gauge.

Note: Graph lines should be drawn on canvas that will be covered completely with stitches. If the background is to be left unworked, mark the dividing lines in soft pencil that can be erased where needed. Pre-test all pens and pencils.

When a design outline is shown in counted stitches, it may be reproduced stitch-by-stitch or placed under the canvas (enlarged if necessary) and outlined in the same manner as a diagram. The geometric lines seem to round out and soften when viewed under a canvas mesh.

How to Enlarge and Transfer Designs

One of the reasons for the enormous popularity of needlepoint on painted canvas is its simplicity. The design is immediately identified as to outline and color placement, and one can relax and concentrate on stitchery.

To transpose a design onto needlepoint canvas, the design must first be transferred to a flat sheet of paper. If the design is shown in actual size, make a photocopy of the page. If the design is shown in sections, photocopy all the sections and assemble them into one design. Tape the design copy to a flat surface, and place the canvas over it. If the lines are not clearly visible, go over them with a black marking pen.

Position the canvas over the paper to center the design, and place a few push pins all around to prevent it from shifting. Allow a proper margin all around: 2" for soft pillows, handbags, and wall hangings; and 3" or more for work to be framed or upholstered. Trace the design outline with a fine-point acrylic pen, outlining shapes, colors, features, etc.

Color in the canvas, using the suggested color key or your personal preference. If you have some artistic ability and would like to create your own design, keep it simple at first. Never place a design directly on canvas without first working it out on paper. Bear in mind that the more complicated the design outlines, the finer the canvas and the smaller the stitches should be.

Any paint can be used as long as it is smudge-proof—by this, I mean any paint, pencils, or colored pens that do not rub off on your hand as you work. No media is completely waterproof, except oil and acrylic paints. Both require a certain amount of artistic training to use properly, and the acrylics will often flake off a heavily sized canvas. Any needlepoint canvas that was painted in oils should never be sent to professional dry cleaners. The solvents used in such cleaning establishments may loosen the oils and bring them to the surface—with disastrous results.

For best results, use acrylic pens or light-colored felt markers. They needn't match the yarns exactly. There is no need to wet needlepoint, as you will see in the instructions for blocking, and professional cleaning will eliminate felt markings without a trace. Pre-test all paints on a scrap of canvas before applying them to actual canvas.

When the design outline is shown reduced in size, the actual dimensions are indicated on the same page. The easiest and most accurate enlarging method is photostating. Check with local newspapers or printing shops for the photostat service nearest you. A photostat is *not* the same as a photocopy. Photocopy machines, available in most libraries and general stores, will duplicate a sheet of paper no larger than legal size. Photostat machines, on the other hand, can enlarge or reduce a design to any size desired. Before enlarging, check the design carefully for any changes you may wish to make. Obliterate unwanted portions with white poster paint, and draw any additions with a black felt-tip marking pen.

The alternative to making a photostat is the old square-by-square method of enlarging. Draw a margin all around the design, and divide the area into sixteen equal squares or rectangles. Do this by measuring and dividing the pattern in half and then quarters, both vertically and horizontally. Take a sheet of paper the size of the proposed enlargement and after outlining the margin, divide it into the same number of squares or rectangles. For a complicated design, subdivide the squares into thirty-two smaller ones. Number the squares in sequence on both the original design and the enlargement paper, and proceed to copy the design square-for-square. The accuracy of the enlargement will depend on individual artistic ability. Remember to make all necessary alterations at this time.

A design may be reduced in size in the same manner that it is enlarged. Make all changes *after* the reduction is completed.

Note: The canvas gauge is indicated in each design outline. You may use a smaller gauge canvas if you wish to work with finer stitches. Do not use a larger mesh canvas unless you enlarge the design in proportion. For example, if a design is to be worked in # 10 canvas and you wish to work in # 5, enlarge the design to double the size indicated in the instruction guide.

When the tracing method of transferring is used on cotton, linen, or any other densely woven fabric, a photostat of an enlarged drawing becomes the master copy. The design must now be copied onto tracing paper, a semi-sheer paper available in art supply stores. It comes in rolls or pads of assorted sizes. If necessary, tape several sheets together with cellophane tape. Place tape-side down on the enlargement, and trace the design outline very carefully with a soft black pencil. Trace on a smooth hard surface, and fasten both papers with push pins to prevent shifting.

The tracing is the working copy, which is used in the final step of design transfer. Press the selected fabric, and tape it to a smooth flat surface. Place a sheet of dressmakers' carbon (transfer paper) shiny-side *down* over the fabric, and position the tracing on top so it is properly centered. Place a few push pins all around, and go over the design outline with a hard pencil. Press firmly to get a clear sharp outline on the fabric.

Transfer paper is sold in dressmaker supplies stores, and it comes in light or dark colors. Do not use typewriter carbon.

Note: If the fabric is too large to be taped down, use paper-weights, heavy books, or felt-covered bricks in several places to keep it flat. If the design has to fit into a special framework and the opaque transfer paper interferes with proper placement, position the tracing and pin it to the fabric on one side. Lift the other side and slide in the transfer paper.

Pre-test transfer paper on a scrap of fabric to make sure the outlines are clear and sharp. Constant lifting and checking as you trace the design may cause the outline to shift.

If your fabric is sheer enough, you can save time by tracing the design directly onto the fabric. Tape the design to a flat surface, and place the sheer fabric over it. Fasten with a few push pins, and trace with a fine indelible or smudge-proof pen. Needlepoint canvas will lie flat, but sheer fabrics, such as organdy, tend to shift and must be secured with extra care. This method will not work on textured fabrics or fabrics with a deep pile because they are not sheer enough to see through.

To transfer a design onto heavier, more textured fabrics, place the fabric on a frame or embroidery hoop (see page 18). Pin or baste the tracing onto the fabric, and stitch the main design outlines through the paper. Peel away the paper, and go over the outlines if necessary. Then fill in the rest of the stitches. Or work the entire design through the paper. If fabric is washable, the paper will disintegrate when washed; otherwise, remove what paper is visible and leave the rest. It will not harm the embroidery.

A tracing can be turned into a hot-iron transfer by outlining it with a Hectograph pencil (see List of Suppliers on pages 119–120). This is a pink wax pencil that may be sharpened like any ordinary pencil for a clear sharp outline. Turn the tracing right-side down, and retrace the entire outline with the Hectograph. Then turn the tracing right-side up, position it onto the fabric, and glide a hot iron over the paper. The resulting outline will be sharp and clear. This method *must* be pre-tested on a small piece of fabric. The temperature of the iron is most important: if it is too cool, the transfer will be unclear; if it is too hot, the outline will smudge. Be careful—an iron that is hot enough to transfer Hectograph may scorch certain fabrics.

If you have the right combination of fabric and temperature, the Hectograph method is quick and easy. The marks are easily removed by dry cleaning, or they can be washed out with soap and water.

Fabric

Needlepoint canvas is the most familiar of the background fabrics. It is an even-weave cotton fabric with open meshes that are easy to count. There are two basic types of canvas: single-thread, or mono; and double thread, or Penelope.

Mono canvas is a simple weave of single vertical and horizontal threads. (Figure 2, A and D.) It comes in stark white as well as a variety of colors and its smooth, flat surface is ideal for tracing and painting designs. Mono canvas is best suited for the Straight Gobelin or Bargello needlework. It is a standard, loosely interwoven fabric with durable threads that can withstand a great deal of wear and tear. It is recommended for large projects, especially those that will be used in upholstery.

There is a new interlocked mono canvas (Figure 2, C) which features smooth, flat threads that do not unravel easily. It is an excellent choice for small projects. The interlocked canvas is not recommended for needlework that requires extensive blocking because the lightweight threads tend to break when stretched.

Double-thread, or Penelope, canvas is the most durable of the needlepoint canvases. (Figure 2, B.) It is excellent for rugs or chairseat covers. In most cases it will outlast the yarn after many years of wear. It is much easier to repair a worn piece of needlework by replacing stitches on a still-durable canvas than it is to insert patches of fresh canvas into a deteriorating background.

The double threads in Penelope may be pushed apart with a needle and worked in finer stitches or petit point. This is especially useful when working a design that has some areas of fine detail, such as facial features, hands, etc.

Penelope canvas is available in gauges up to # $3^1/_2$, which is sometimes known as quick-point canvas.

A canvas of good quality is firm but not rigid. The mesh threads run straight and true, and the knots that re-tie broken threads are far apart and barely visible.

Freshly unrolled canvas may seem a little crooked, but a good tug at opposite corners should straighten it out. A very firm canvas that resists the tug may be relaxed by giving it a light steaming and then pulling it back into shape before it dries and regains its firmness.

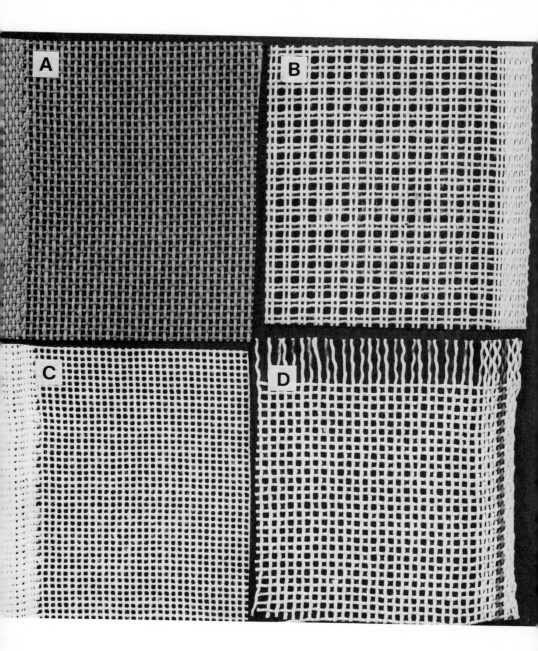

FIGURE 2

A, # 12 Mono canvas (interwoven) in tan; B, # 5 Double thread canvas in white (suitable for rugs); C, # 12 Mono canvas (interlocked); D, # 10 Mono canvas (interwoven) with raveled threads. Finished edges are called selvedge.

11

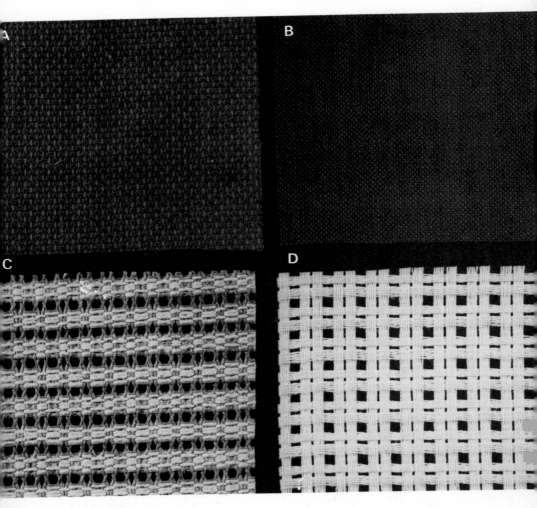

FIGURE 3

A, Aida even-weave cotton; B, Linda fine even-weave cotton; C, Rya cloth; D, Demo double mesh light-weight novelty cloth.

Needlepoint canvas is always coated with a special starch called sizing. This gives it body and a firm support for stitches. An open-mesh cotton fabric would otherwise be limp, and the mesh threads would lose their form under the pressure of the heavy yarns. The stitches would look uneven and the over-all effect would be unattractive.

Starched, or sized, fabric is essential for all work that will require blocking. In the blocking process, a distorted canvas is pulled back into shape and nailed to a board. The sizing is softened by steaming. As it dries, it regains its firmness as well as its original shape. (For more information, see the chapter on blocking.)

Canvas is sold by gauge number. The gauge is the number of meshes, or threads, within a linear inch. The greater the number of threads, the finer the canvas holes. Ask for canvas by number and type of weave: # 10 mono canvas is a single-thread canvas with ten meshes to the inch.

Canvas is available in a wide selection of colors in addition to the standard white and tan. A novelty color is desirable only when large portions of the canvas fabric are to be left unworked. Otherwise, use white for needlework with light colored yarns and tan for projects with darker yarns.

Stark white canvas will sometimes show through black or very dark backgrounds. If tan canvas is not available, tint the white canvas with tea or coffee. Pour a medium-strength solution of cooled tea or coffee into a basin. Dip the canvas for a few minutes, and then dry it on a flat surface. If the canvas is wrinkled, press it with a hot iron over a damp cloth. The stain will be a uniform tan color. Be sure to cool the liquid before dipping your canvas. If the liquid is hot, it will wash away the sizing, leaving your canvas limp.

If the canvas does become limp, however, you can renew its freshness with some spray starch and a light ironing. If the canvas becomes limp while you are working on it, steam press on the reverse side and let it dry. If this does not seem to help, cover the reverse side with a light cotton cloth, spray it with starch, and press over it. Let dry before resuming work.

Aida (Figure 3, A) is a fine even-weave cotton cloth that resembles monk's cloth. It is available in a variety of colors and gauges and is excellent for counted-stitch work as well as for embroidery.

Linda (Figure 3, B) is a very fine, even-weave cotton cloth that is less costly than linen. It comes in over two dozen fresh colors and 42" width.

Rya cloth (Figure 3, C) is a specially woven fabric for Rya or

Turkish knots. Open mesh and closely woven rows alternate to create even spacing between the rows of loops. Rya is a durable fabric and makes an excellent background for the heaviest looped rugs. It comes in 36" width and in gray only.

Demo (Figure 3, D) is a wide open double-mesh cloth. It is not as durable as standard Penelope rug canvas, nor is it as heavily sized, but it does provide a beautiful backing for heavy craft yarns worked in large textured stitches. Demo does not need complete coverage. It is available in several colors that intermingle nicely with contrasting yarns.

The above fabrics may be purchased at most needlework shops, or see the List of Suppliers on pages 119–120.

Mending Torn Canvas

Needlepoint canvas should be handled gently. But even the most careful needleworker may have to cope with a torn canvas. If the

FIGURE 4

canvas is worked in the area of the tear, pick out enough stitches to bare several mesh holes all around. If the tear occurs in an unworked area, stitch several lines around it. Pull out the broken canvas threads both ways, and pull them through the stitches on the reverse side with a thin crochet hook. Remove a few canvas threads from the outer edge and, threading them through a needle, darn the hole by weaving vertically and horizontally. (Figure 4.) Fasten the tail ends into the worked canvas on the reverse side.

This method of mending canvas is applicable to *interwoven* canvas only. Interlocked canvas must be patched. To do this, cut a piece of canvas large enough to extend 1" all around the torn area. Trim the hole into an even square or rectangle. Place the patch under the opening, being careful to line up all the meshes. Baste with thread that matches the canvas and work your stitches through both pieces, extending about 1" around the damaged part. Cut away any excess on the other side.

Yarns

Needlepoint yarns come in a wide variety of colors and textures. The yarns used in canvas work must be strong enough to withstand the pull through the canvas without fraying.

Persian yarn is the most popular and practical needlepoint yarn. It is all wool and is available in an enormous selection of colors. Persian yarn is made of three strands (plies), which separate easily and may be adapted to any size mesh by adding or removing one or more plies. Subtle shadings can be achieved by blending two or more shades.

English crewel is also a multi-ply wool yarn. It is somewhat thinner than the Persian type and may require an extra strand of yarn to cover a given canvas.

Tapestry yarn is a four-ply twist that does not separate into single plies. It is excellent for any needlework but only fits some canvas gauges, usually # 10 and sometimes # 12. Pre-test on a piece of canvas before beginning a large project.

Silk is one of the most beautiful needlepoint materials. The English silk is a little more shiny than the French, and it has a tendency to fray. French silk has a beautiful satin luster and is very nice to work with. Add small amounts of silk for highlights and a touch of elegance.

Six-strand embroidery floss is a soft and manageable cotton thread that comes in many colors and may be used to highlight small areas. It soils easily and should not be worked over a large area, unless the needlework is washable.

There are a number of needlepoint yarns made from synthetic fibers. They do not come in as many colors as wool yarns, and they have a tendency to mat after a time. However, they are washable, non-allergic, and often less expensive than wool.

Renewing Yarn Texture

Yarn may become matted for a number of reasons. The strands look fuzzy and they seem to stick together. When this occurs, soak the yarn in Woolite and cool water for a few minutes and then squeeze the moisture out by running your fingers along the strands. Let dry over a towel.

Tools and Supplies

Needles. Needles come in a large variety of specialized shapes and sizes. They are divided into two general categories: sharp-pointed, such as crewel and darners for work on densely woven fabrics, and blunt-pointed (tapestry) needles for open weaves such as canvas or net. Needles must be compatible with both the fabric and the working yarns. Purchase them by size (gauge). The finer the needle the larger its number. Needles are distributed under different brand names, and although the eye gauge is fairly constant, the length of the shaft may vary. Find the length that is most comfortable in your hand.

Thimbles. Thimbles are a matter of personal preference. Some needles slide through canvas so easily that it is not always necessary to use a thimble. But if you use one, select one that fits comfortably.

Scissors. Two pairs of scissors are a must: one small, sharp-pointed pair that fits into small areas to rip stitches or to cut yarn ends; and a large pair to cut canvas and other fabric.

Tape. Tape is another necessity. It should be the self-adhesive masking tape available in hardware stores. A 1" width is adequate. Fold it over the cut edge of the canvas to prevent the threads from ravelling and to make the canvas easier to handle.

A **ruler** or measuring tape should also be part of your needlework "tool box," as well as some fine-point acrylic **marking pens**, and a small **magnet** to pick up stray pins and needles.

Hoops and Frames. A frame or a hoop can be very useful in learning to work a variety of embroidery stitches. It is, of course, possible to work without a frame, but the number of stitches you can work would then be reduced. The main function of an embroidery frame or hoop is to stretch the fabric and keep it taut while working the stitches. The stitches will look more even and require less blocking.

There is a large selection of hoops and frames available wherever needlepoint supplies are sold. (Figure 5.) The hoops are either round or oval, and the frames are rectangular with adjustable sides. The best ones can be anchored to a stand, leaving both hands free.

The round hoops that fasten to a simple floor stand are excellent for small projects. The stands adjust to different heights, and the hoops are interchangeable. Therefore, you can leave a piece of work on one hoop while trying out some stitches on another. Some hoops screw onto a tabletop, and others are attached to a small platform one can sit on. *It is largely a matter of personal preference.*

Round (hoop) frames come in two parts; one seamless ring fits inside a larger one that adjusts with a special screw. To mount the fabric onto a round hoop, adjust the screw on the outer ring so that it fits tightly over the inner ring and fabric. Pull the fabric all around until it is taut. Then push the outer ring down. To release the fabric, press both thumbs on the fabric at the edge of the frame while lifting the outer ring.

Square frames are ideal for larger pieces of work. The width is usually standard from 18" to 36" but the length is adjusted on rollers at both ends. The rollers have strips of tape stapled across them. The side of the fabric that does not exceed the length of the strip is sewn to the tape at both ends. If the fabric is longer than

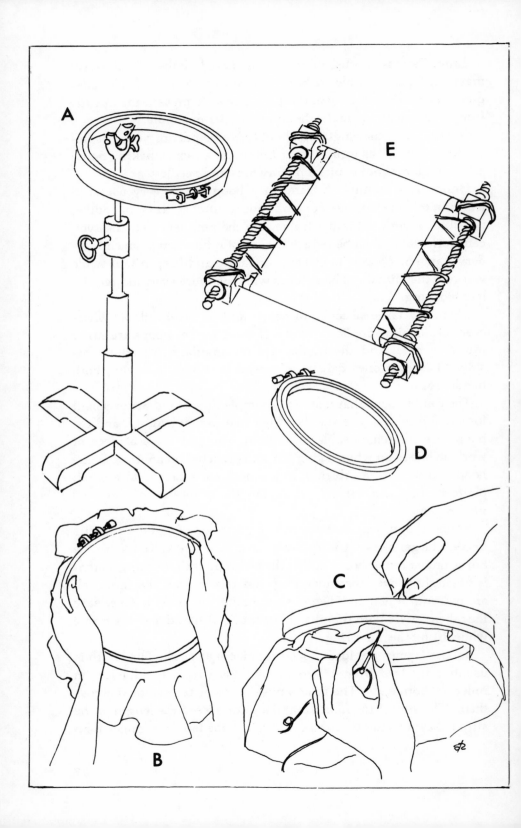

A

E

D

B

C

the distance between the rollers, wind the surplus neatly over one roller. Lace the sides as shown in Figure E. If the sides of the needlepoint fabric do not have a heavy-duty selvage, stitch a length of tape or special stitch webbing at either side before lacing.

When the embroidery on this portion of fabric is completed, the lacing is removed, the finished embroidery is rolled up at one end, and fresh fabric is unrolled at the other end. The sides are then laced again.

On any frame, the stitches should be worked in an up-and-down motion, not in a sewing motion. Always keep one hand below the frame and the other hand above. Each hand receives the needle as it is pushed by the other hand through the fabric. It takes a little practice, but the technique is simple once mastered.

When learning the stitch construction, especially of looped and knotted stitches, work in "slow motion" so that each step is clearly defined, and notice when and how the yarn is looped around the needle. This will make it easier to work on a frame.

Note: Never crowd the embroidery inside the frame. Allow at least 2" of space between the embroidery outline and the framework.

FIGURE 5

A, Floor stand with hoop frame; B, Mounting fabric into a round hoop frame; C, Proper hand position when working with embroidery frame; D, Hoop frame with seamless ring inside larger ring with screw; E, Square frame with laced sides.

XXX

COMBINATION STITCHES

The stitch patterns in this chapter are created with a combination of two or more of the basic upright, slanted, or looped stitches. Starting on page 40 you will find projects worked in a combination of stitch techniques. Included also are a number of needlework designs worked in a combination of stitch techniques over partial areas to create a combination of *stitcheries* and to show the compatibility of stitches and stitch formations from the three basic categories. A more complete guide to these simple stitches—including projects and designs—is available in three books: *Mira Silverstein's Guide to Upright Stitches, Mira Silverstein's Guide to Slanted Stitches,* and *Mira Silverstein's Guide to Looped and Knotted Stitches.*

Double Cross Stitch Pattern

The Double Cross is a large stitch pattern constructed of two crosses, one diagonal and one straight. (Figure 6.) The straight cross is worked first. The threaded needle comes up at 1, goes in at 2, comes up at 3, and goes back in at 4. The second cross is worked diagonally over the first one. It does not matter which diagonal stitch is placed first, but in close formation the last stitch should always be worked in the same direction for a uniform texture.

The stitch pattern is diamond shaped and may be worked in groups of larger diamonds in varying colors. (Figure 7.)

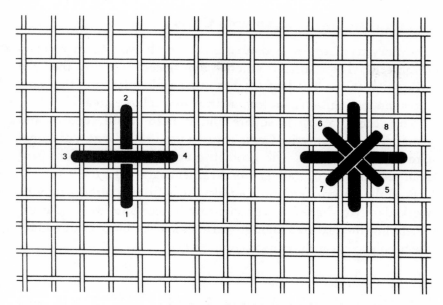

FIGURE 6   Double Cross Stitch Detail

FIGURE 7   Double Cross Stitch Pattern

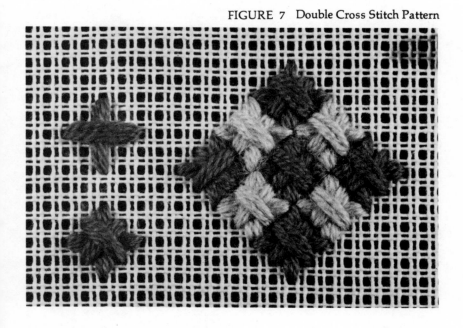

Smyrna Cross

The Smyrna Cross is a double cross stitch worked in reverse. (Figure 8.) The diagonal stitches are placed first and then the straight stitches. The last stitches must all be placed in the same direction to maintain a uniform texture over a large area.

The stitch pattern is square and is used to fill squares and rectangles. The Smyrna Cross is often used to enlarge a diagonal Cross Stitch pattern. The geometric outline becomes more pronounced, and the overall texture is rather coarse. (Figure 9.)

Both the Smyrna and the Double Cross Stitch patterns may be worked in two shades, but special care is necessary to avoid overwhelming the texture. Enough yarn should be used in threading the needle to cover the canvas completely.

FIGURE 9 Smyrna Stitch Pattern

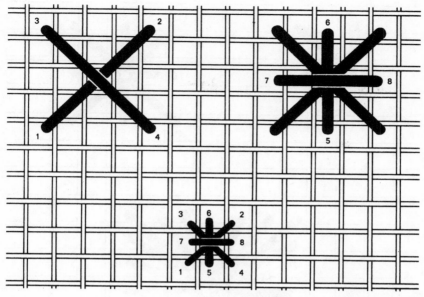

FIGURE 8   Smyrna Stitch Detail

Algerian Eye Stitch Pattern

The Algerian Eye is a versatile stitch pattern that may be worked in a square or diamond shape. It looks as well in fine embroidery thread with some of the fabric showing as it does in heavy yarn that covers the canvas completely with the exception of the small center eye.

The stitch detail in Figure 10 shows the Algerian Eye in three different patterns. The threaded needle comes up at the odd numbers and goes in at the even. The needle is constantly carried through the same center opening. The center should become clearly visible. If the fabric is too firm, push the point of closed embroidery scissors through the center and twist to enlarge the eye. Be careful not to cut the fabric threads; simply push them apart.

Algerian Eyes are very striking when worked on a large background. Place them singly or in small clusters in random areas. Match the color of the background fabric (Figure 11) but use threads of different texture—both matte and shiny.

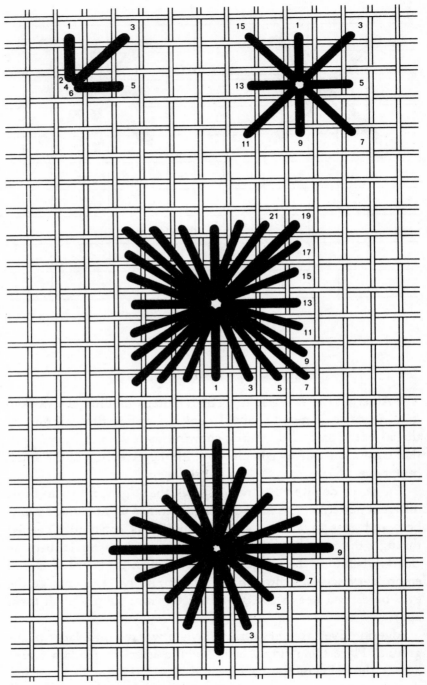

FIGURE 10   Algerian Eye Stitch Detail

FIGURE 11
Algerian Stitch (Square and Diamond Patterns)

Leviathan Stitch Pattern

The Leviathan is a bulky cross stitch somewhat heavier than the Smyrna and the Double Cross. The line stitches seem to radiate around the center but, unlike the Algerian Eye, the stitches cross over the center point, creating a slight pyramid instead of an opening. (Figure 12.)

Work the first two diagonal lines with the threaded needle coming up at 1, going in at 2, coming up at 3, and going in at 4. Continue with the needle coming up at odd numbers and going in at even ones. Notice that the stitches are not worked in a circle, but each diagonal line is crossed over separately. Numbers 1–2 are crossed with 5–6 and 7–8. Numbers 4–5 are crossed with 9–10 and 11–12.

Finish with a straight cross. It is shown in contrasting color (Figure 13) but it may be worked in the same shade as the rest of the stitch pattern. The Leviathan is a versatile stitch pattern that covers well and looks very handsome on large open-mesh canvas.

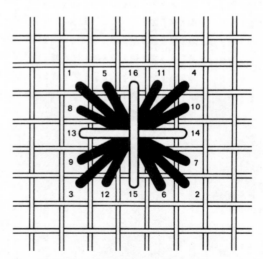

FIGURE 12   Leviathan Stitch Detail

FIGURE 13
Leviathan Stitch Patterns

Spider Web Stitch Patterns

The Spider Webs are woven stitches. A framework is placed on the surface of the fabric, and the threaded needle weaves in and out in a circle, filling the frame like a spider web.

There are several types of Spider Web Stitch patterns. The two shown here are the easiest to work and are very handy when a rounded stitch pattern is needed.

To create the Spider Web in Figure 14, make a group of stitches like the spokes of a wheel. You need an *uneven* number of spokes, and it may be necessary to measure and pencil them in to make sure they are evenly distributed. Use a blunt tapestry needle, and work the spokes through the center and over and under the canvas or fabric.

After the spokes have been placed, come up through the center and weave the needle in and out of the spokes and round and round to the edge. Do not pull the weaving thread too tight. The finished stitch pattern is round, raised near the outer edge and depressed in the center. Figure 15 shows a variation of this Spider Web.

To create the Spider Web in Figure 16, use any number of spokes. Begin at the center and weave the circle by going under each spoke and then returning to go over it in a wrap-around motion. Work in a circle up to the edge, or leave part of the spokes showing for a sun-ray effect. The spokes should be covered with ridges with flat stitches between them.

FIGURE 14
Spider Web Stitch Detail and Pattern

FIGURE 15
Spider Web Stitch Pattern
decorating a small box

FIGURE 16
Spider Web Stitch Detail and Pattern

Leaf Stitch Pattern

The Leaf Stitch is not difficult to learn, but the line stitches must be counted very carefully so that they meet at the proper mesh squares. Practice on large open-mesh canvas to better understand the construction of this pattern. (Figure 17.)

Begin at the top and come up at 1 with threaded needle. Go in at 2 and continue with an over-and-under motion, coming up at the odd numbers and going in at the even. Follow numerical order carefully and after the stem 23–24 is completed, work to the left and begin the new point at 25–26.

Practice larger and smaller leaf patterns. The stem 23–24 is shown in a contrasting color in Figure 18 to make it clearly visible. The texture of the Leaf Stitch is very attractive. By working the stems in a different color, you emphasize these little vertical lines, giving a striped effect to the overall design.

To mix colors in the Leaf Stitch pattern, alternate shades at random or at regular intervals.

FIGURE 17
Leaf Stitch Detail

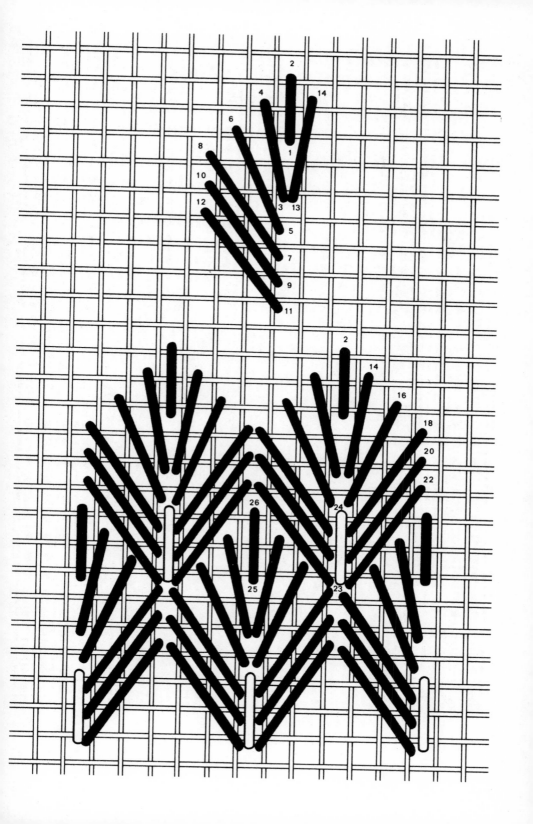

FIGURE 18   Leaf Stitch Pattern

Rhodes (Pyramid) Stitch Pattern

The Rhodes is a large, textured block stitch pattern that can be worked over any number of canvas threads. It looks most attractive as a larger unit because the accumulation of layers of yarn in the center creates a dome or pyramid. (Figure 19.)

Decide on the overall dimension of the stitch unit, and place the first diagonal stitch as a line between points 1 and 2. Go in at 2 (under the canvas), and come up at 3 (to the right of 1), go across to 4 (to the left of 2), and come out at 5.

This multi-stitch unit is easier to read in numbered diagram rather than in stitch detail. The diagram is shown in three sizes. The threaded needle comes up at the lower-left corner and ends on the stitch above the starting point. The needle comes up at odd numbers and goes in at even numbers.

Rhodes Stitches are worked over and under the canvas in a counter-clockwise direction. The upper line moves to the left as the lower line moves to the right, and the right line moves upward as the left line moves downward. Relax the working yarn so that it piles up in a center dome. (Figure 20, A.)

The stitch units, worked in rows, will show bare canvas threads around the edges. (Figure 20, B.) These can be covered with lines of back stitches. (Figure 20, C.) To create an overlay of diamonds in a contrasting color, work the Rhodes Stitch pattern over an even number of canvas squares.

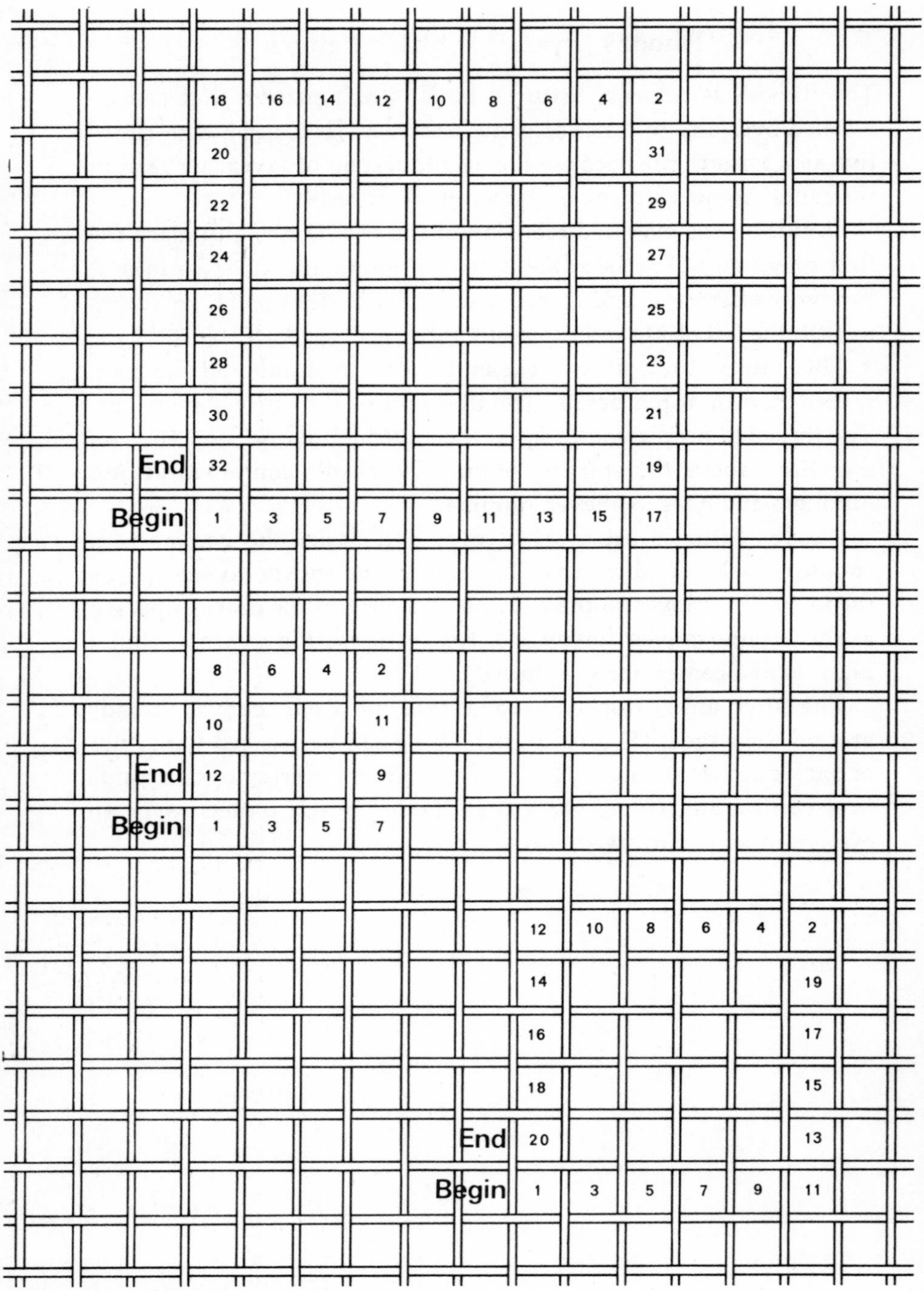

18   16   14   12   10   8   6   4   2

20   31

22   29

24   27

26   25

28   23

30   21

End 32   19

Begin 1   3   5   7   9   11   13   15   17

8   6   4   2

10   11

End 12   9

Begin 1   3   5   7

12   10   8   6   4   2

14   19

16   17

18   15

End 20   13

Begin 1   3   5   7   9   11

FIGURE 19   Rhodes Stitch Detail

FIGURE 20
Rhodes Stitch Pattern

A

B   C

Couching

Couching is a stitching method used in needlework to fasten decorative yarns or threads which are too heavy or brittle to be stitched in the conventional manner.

Heavy cord, ribbon, and metallic threads are usually couched. The material to be couched is inserted at one end of the line through an opening in the fabric enlarged with the closed points on embroidery scissors. A threaded needle comes up at that point and fastens the cord or metallic thread with small stitches. These stitches may be straight or crossed, in matching or contrasting colors.

Couching stitches should be evenly spaced and pulled just enough to hold the couched material in place without distorting it. To make decorative couched designs, draw the outlines on the fabric and guide the cord along these lines with your left hand while stitching with your right. Couching must be worked on a hoop or embroidery frame (see page 18).

Figure 21 illustrates several samples of couching: straight, serpentine, and round lines.

Long and Short Stitches

The Long and Short Stitches, as their name implies, are stitches of varying lengths used to fill an open area when a flat untextured effect is desired. These stitches are excellent for shading because the stitches encroach slightly. The Long and Short Stitches are combination stitches because they are generally worked in all directions.

Shown in enlarged detail on the partridge (page 63), the Long and Short Stitches are all vertical. They are worked in close formation to create a smooth even-textured background.

Long and Short Stitches take on a different appearance in the flowers on color page C3. The stitches are bold, worked at random, and overlapped in some places.

Flowers like these may be worked over a background of Tent Stitches.

FIGURE 21
Couching with Detail

XX

PROJECTS

Counted-stitch Precolumbian Design

This is a very simple geometric pattern that may be worked as a single ornament for a denim jacket or as a repeat pattern for a handsome rug bordered with a compatible border.

Each unit is a Double Cross Stitch worked over # 10 mesh canvas. It may be enlarged with larger cross stitches like the Double Leviathan on a large gauge canvas. Begin at the center and work one side and then the other. (Figures 22 and 23.)

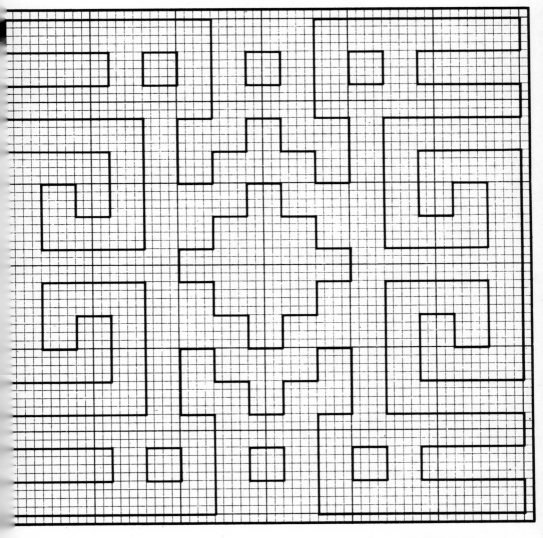

FIGURE 22

FIGURE 23

Bargello and Basketweave

Work the Bargello pattern in Figure 24 in three shades of one color. Fill the background with Basketweave in the lightest value of the color or leave it unfinished.

Work on # 12 mono canvas. You will need 2 yards of each shade for every pattern unit as shown in Figure 25 and 2 yards for every square inch of basketweave.

FIGURE 24

FIGURE 25

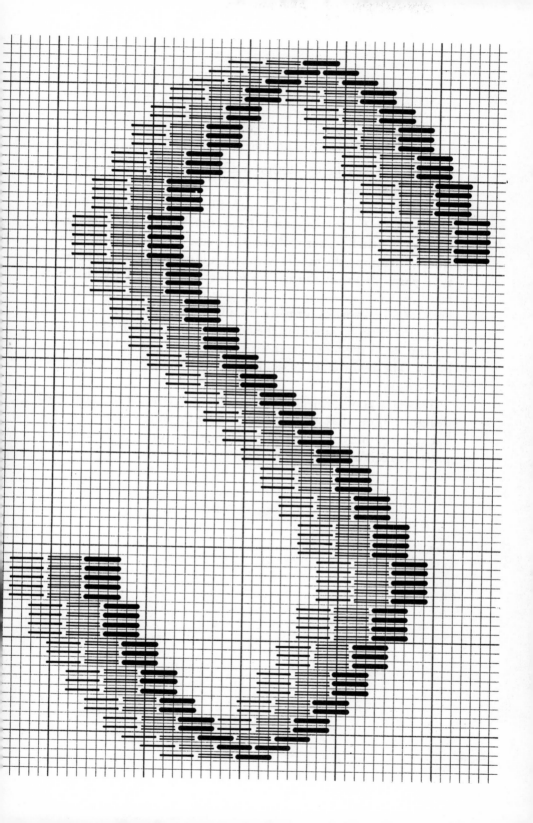

Lion

MATERIALS: 10" x 12" # 10 mono canvas (includes 2" margin)
1 oz. (about 40 yards) background color
1 oz. medium gold
8 yards each of light gold, dark gold, and black for outline.

Trace and enlarge the design outline in Figure 26 according to general instructions on page 6.

Work the outline in black, then fill in the body and head in Diagonal Tent or Basketweave. Next, finish the background in the Cashmere Stitch pattern. Work the mane and tail tip in Turkish Knots, threading the needle with two full triple strands of Persian-type yarn. Begin at the neck and work rows of Turkish Knots three canvas threads apart. Alternate the shades of gold at random. Mix two shades, or use dark and light separately.

Fill the entire area within the dotted outline with Turkish Knots 2" long. Clip the loops, and brush the mane and tail with a stiff brush. The two shades of gold will blend and look very effective. (Figure 27.)

This is a good project for a beginner. It is a simple unshaded design outline that shows three separate stitch patterns. The background may be worked in almost any other kind of stitch pattern or left unfinished.

FIGURE 26

FIGURE 27

Tennis Racquet Cover

(See color page C2.)

This is a geometric design worked in Diagonal Cross Stitch and Algerian Eye Stitch patterns. It is worked on the blank # 12 interlocked canvas of a prefabricated tennis racquet cover. Divide the canvas in half and in quarters with light pencil lines. Beginning at the center, follow the graph in Figure 28 to work out the first pattern.

MATERIALS: One tennis racquet cover (see List of Suppliers pages 119–120)
One 8-yard skein of green Persian-type yarn
Two 8-yard skeins of navy Persian-type yarn
Two 8-yard skeins of magenta Persian-type yarn

Work Algerian Eye in single ply, the Cross Stitch in two plies, and place a single Double Cross in the center of each pattern (see graph) in single ply. Do not fill in background. (Figures 28 and 29.)

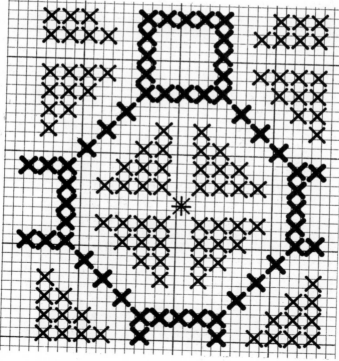

FIGURE 28

49

FIGURE 29   Enlarged detail for Tennis Racquet Cover *(see color page 2, Bottom, A)*

Small Make-up Bag

This is a prefabricated travel bag with zipper and painted canvas. (Figure 30.) It is available in a kit, complete with yarn. Stitch the buckle (Figure 31) in Basketweave and the background in straight Gobelin.

MATERIALS: Small bag (see List of Suppliers pages 119–120)
One 8-yard skein of red Persian-type yarn for belt
One 8-yard skein of yellow Persian-type yarn
Two 8-yard skeins of tan Persian-type yarn

Victor's Pillow

This is an interesting design using the simplest stitches. (Figure 32.) Make the canvas any size. Draw letters free-hand or count stitches. The letters are worked in Basketweave Stitch. Work the rest of the pillow in stripes created with Hungarian Stitch patterns in random colors. To finish pillow see instructions on pages 117–118.

FIGURE 30

FIGURE 31

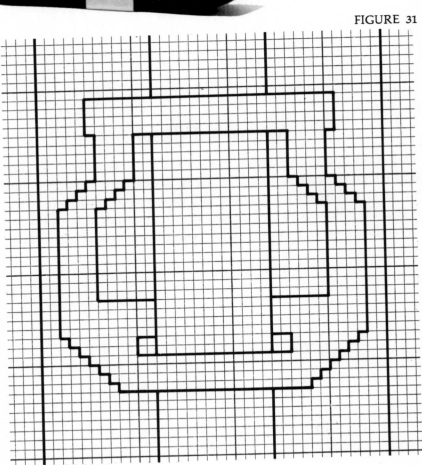

FIGURE 32

Handbag

(See color page C2.)

This is a needlepoint worked in stripes of different patterns. The unfinished canvas is photographed in black and white (Figure 33) and may be enlarged and used for a number of projects.

The actual dimensions are 12″ × 24″. This is an ideal size for an envelope purse. Any of the pattern stripes may also be copied and made into belts. Or you can use a small portion of the pattern to create a pillow.

This design was worked in Chain, Long and Short, Straight, Fishbone, Gobelin, and Tent Stitches.

MATERIALS: 14″ × 26″ piece of # 12 interlocked mono canvas (includes a 2″ margin all around)
Two small 8-yard skeins of Persian-type yarn in colors indicated in color photograph

Study Figures 33 and 34. Work design in Basketweave or assorted stitches. The flowers are outlined in Chain Stitches and filled in with Straight Stitches. The small red flowers are worked in Long and Short random stitches with an unfinished background.

An envelope handbag should be finished professionally.

54

FIGURE 33

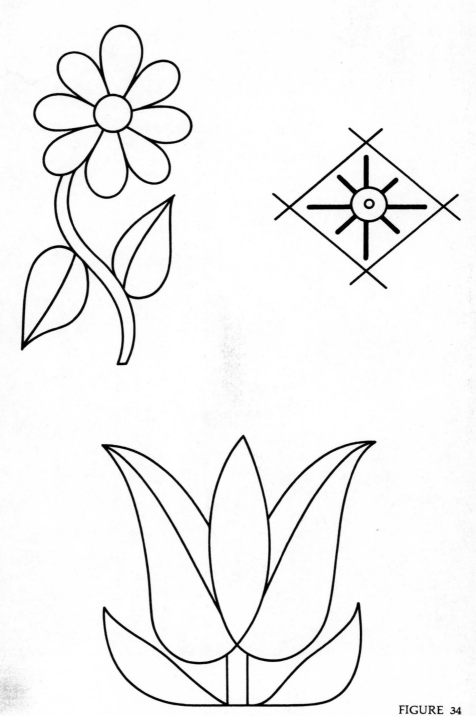

FIGURE 34
Diagrams for Envelope Handbag (see color page 2, Bottom, C)

Top: Partridge in a Tree (Figures 35–40).

Bottom: Small Stylized Birds (Figures 41–43).

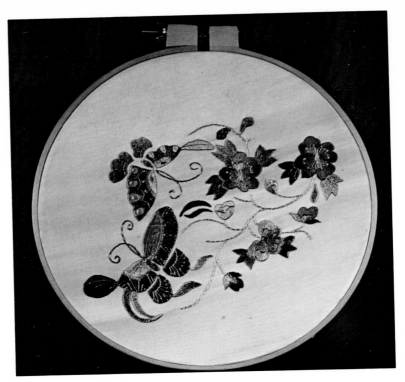

Top: Chinese Butterflies (Figures 45–47).

Bottom: A, Tennis Racquet Cover courtesy Toni Totes, Inc. (Figures 28 and 29); B, Little Scarecrow Name Plaque (Figures 57–59); C, Envelope Handbag (Figures 33 and 34).

Top: Lady with Pickle Jars (Figures 61–66).

Bottom: Flower Bouquet worked in free-form Long and Short Stitches (Page 38) and French Knots (Figure 83).

Top: Log Cabin Patchwork (Figures 48–53).

Bottom: Noah's Ark Scene available through Cute and Custom (see List of Suppliers).

Partridge in a Tree

(See color page C1.)

MATERIALS: Medium-weight embroidery linen or comparable fabric for background 22" × 28" (includes a 3" fold-back margin all around)
Assorted colors of crewel yarn (see color photograph)
Crewel needle

This crewel needlework is shown in actual size. (Figures 35, 36, 37 and 38.) The design outline is divided into four parts. To assemble, trace each page on tracing paper, line up the letters A through E and tape. Figures 39 and 40 show the partridge in black and white.

Press the fabric and transfer the design onto it according to the general transferring instructions on pages 6–9. Use transfer paper or the hot-iron method.

There should be at least a 2" border around the bird outline. Embroider with Satin Stitch, Long and Short Stitches, Stem Stitch, Buttonhole Stitch, French Knots, and Chain Stitch outline as indicated in diagram.

Embroideries of this kind are generally worked on a frame. But this can be worked successfully in the hand because the stitches are short and the Chain Stitch outlines will cover any uneven spots around the edges. (For blocking instructions, see page 114.)

Note: Stitches and colors may be changed if you wish. Similar clear-cut patterns may be copied from greeting cards, children's story books, or coloring books.

Stitch Guide for Partridge in a Tree

1. Long and Short Stitch (head, body, and apples)
2. Satin Stitch (eye, beak, feathers, leaves, branch and claws)
3. Cross Stitch (neckband outlines with Chain Stitch)
4. Buttonhole, Feather Stitch, and French Knots worked in vertical rows.

The outer outlines around the bird, the apples, the branch, wing, claws, and center design are in Chain Stitch. The outlines in and around the leaves are in Stem Stitch. The small stitches inside the wing feathers and inside the claws are Back Stitch.

FIGURE 35

Actual-size diagram for Partridge in a Tree (see color page 1, Top).
Trace and align A–A, B–B, C–C, D–D, E–E for full pattern.

E—

FIGURE 36

FIGURE 37

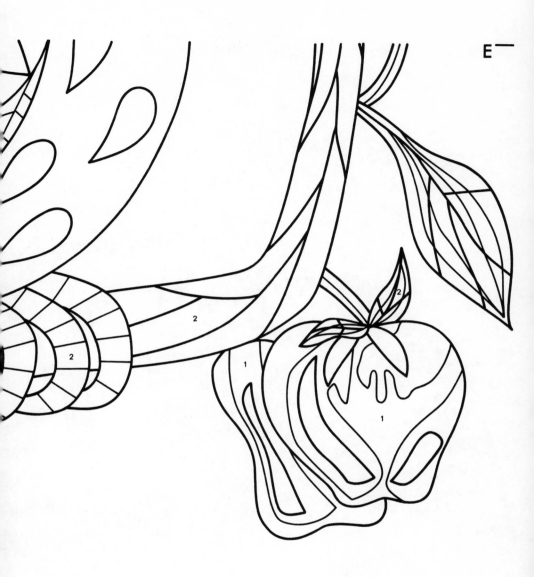

E—

FIGURE 38

FIGURE 39

FIGURE 40

Small Stylized Birds

(See color page C1.)

This is one simple pattern worked in a variety of stitches and colors. It is a very good project to utilize leftover lengths of yarn and thread.

The stitch patterns used are Algerian Eye, Scottish, Leaf, Cross, Double Cross as well as Brick, Straight Gobelin, and Basketweave (Diagonal Tent). Some black beads were placed in the eye detail to add highlights in a large plain black circle.

Two of the birds have a slightly different tail, which is indicated in Figure 41.

As an exercise in creative stitchery, work up as many bird samples as possible in assorted stitches. Make a wall hanging in a variation on one pattern. (Figures 42 and 43.)

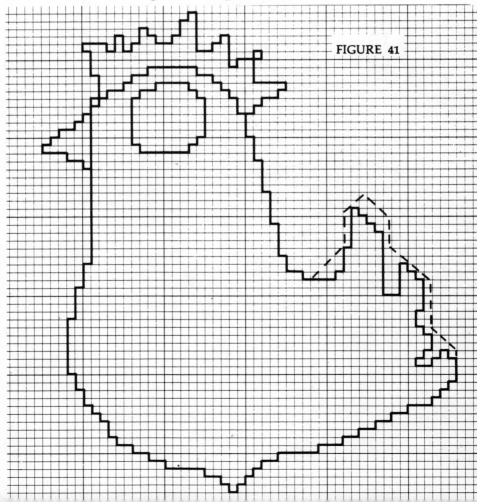

FIGURE 41

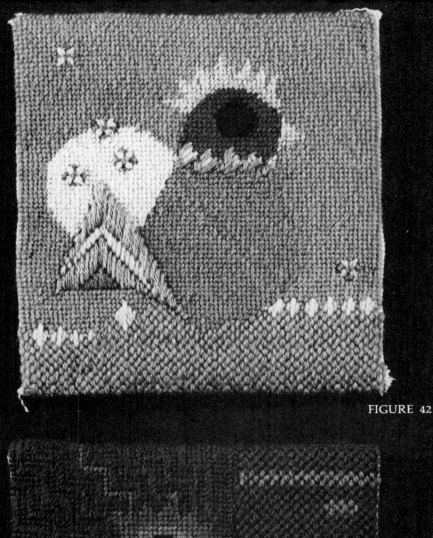

FIGURE 42

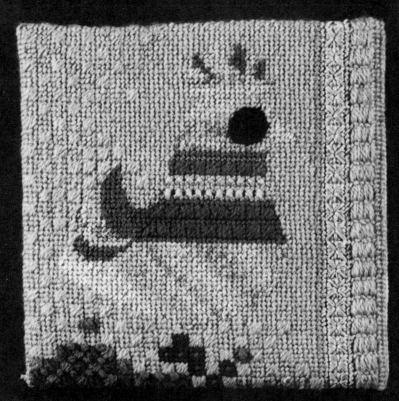

FIGURE 43

Chinese Butterflies

(See color page C2.)

This design is worked in laid work. It is an interesting if time-consuming needlework. In laid work, very long stitches are placed parallel to one another, close enough to cover an open area. These stitches are not worked in an over-and-under motion but are carried back and forth across the fabric. (Figure 44.)

The needle comes up at the bottom line, is carried across to the top line, brought up to the right of the top stitch, and carried across to the bottom line. Skip a space as you work left to right, and fill in the skipped space on the return row as you work right to left.

Working in this manner keeps the outline smooth and even. When the areas are filled with a layer of long stitches, they are held down with a number of small holding stitches. Work laid work on a frame or hoop.

The butterflies are shown in Figures 45 and 46. Photocopy or trace each part and assemble as indicated.

MATERIALS: Tightly woven untextured fabric to accommodate design plus a 3" fold-back margin
Cotton embroidery floss in assorted colors for butterflies and flowers (see color photograph)

Transfer the design onto fabric according to the general transfer directions on pages 6–9. Stretch on a hoop or frame (page 18) and stitch one shape at a time. Work the smaller areas in Satin Stitches, the stems in Stem Stitches, and the butterfly antenae in Double Running Stitches. (Figure 47.)

To work the holding stitches or laid work, trace the butterflies and the flowers on very thin tissue paper and pin the tracings over the appropriate areas that have been filled in with the long stitches. Place the pins outside the design outlines and work the holding stitches such as Stem, Fly and Back Stitches through the paper and the fabric. Peel away the paper and go over some stitches if necessary.

Holding stitches are usually worked free-hand. But if you are a beginner, a tissue paper tracing is very helpful.

FIGURE 47

Close-up of laid work for Chinese Butterflies
and Flowers (see color page 2, Top).

FIGURE 44   Laid Work Detail

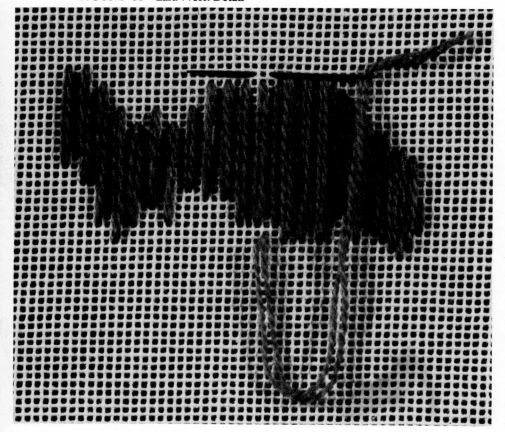

A

FIGURE 45

B

70

FIGURE 46

Chinese Butterflies and Flowers (see color page 2, Top).
Trace and align A–A, B–B for full pattern.

71

Log Cabin Patchwork

(See color page C4.)

The finished size is 16" × 16". This is a needlepoint adaptation of an Early American patchwork pattern. The Log Cabin pattern consists of a number of narrow strips sewn around a center square. The strips become progressively longer as they form a square block. (Figure 48.)

The strips within each block are divided into light and dark colors, and it is this division of colors and block placement that creates the interesting pattern of the Log Cabin.

The patches were simulated in needlepoint in a wide variety of stitch patterns and color combinations. No two strips are exactly alike.

MATERIALS: 18" × 18" mono canvas # 14
Persian yarns in light and dark shades

Each center is a 1" square worked on 14 canvas threads in width and in length. Each patch or strip is ½" (seven canvas threads) wide. The strips increase in length by half an inch as you work from center to border. Figure 48 shows the outline for each individual block. Figure 49 shows the schematic outline of the placement of blocks within the entire design.

Divide the canvas into 16 squares (four across and four down). (Figure 49.) Allow 56 canvas threads both horizontally and vertically.

Work out each block unit separately, beginning with its own center square over fourteen canvas threads. Create each needlepoint pattern on the strips, over seven canvas threads only.

The stitches are clearly visible in color on page 4, Top and in the four enlarged details in Figures 50, 51, 52, and 53. It is not necessary to duplicate all the stitch patterns. Try creating your own combinations. The important thing is to keep the pattern seven canvas threads in width and the light and dark color divisions as indicated in the diagram and color photograph.

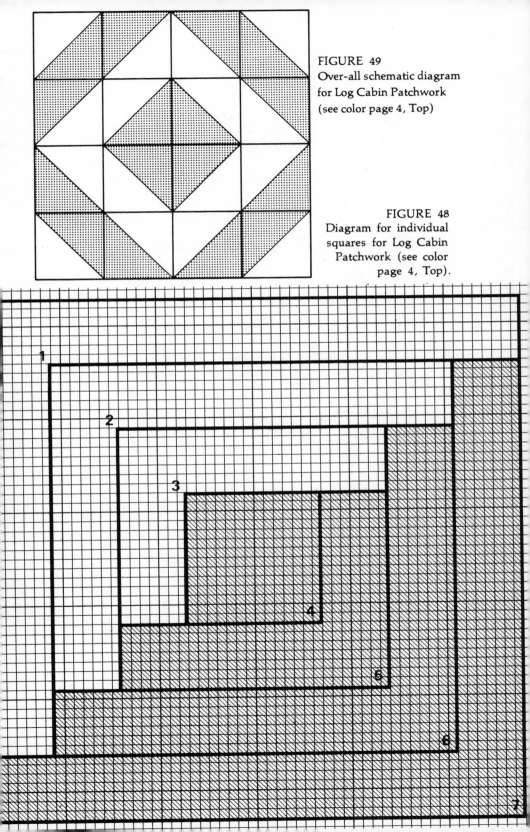

FIGURE 49
Over-all schematic diagram
for Log Cabin Patchwork
(see color page 4, Top)

FIGURE 48
Diagram for individual
squares for Log Cabin
Patchwork (see color
page 4, Top).

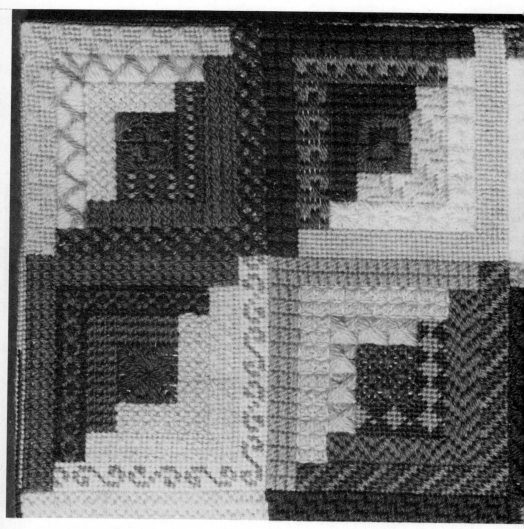

FIGURE 50
Log Cabin Patchwork, upper left corner

FIGURE 51
Log Cabin Patchwork, upper right corner

FIGURE 52
Log Cabin Patchwork, lower left corner

FIGURE 53

Log Cabin Patchwork, lower right corner

Bicycle Seat Cover

MATERIALS: One square of # 12 mono canvas to accommodate the entire outline of the bicycle seat cover plus a 2" margin all around. One 8-yard skein Persian-type yarn each—white, black, yellow, blue, and magenta
1 oz. blue-green yarn for background
3/4 yard denim or duck
1 yard cotton cord or shoe lace

Place a sheet of paper over the seat cover and pencil the outline. Fold paper in half, lengthwise, and even out the outline. Add 1" all around and trace it on a square of canvas. Enlarge or reduce the bee (Figure 54) according to general directions on pages 6–9 and trace it on the center of the bicycle seat outline.

Work the bee in Diagonal Tent (Basketweave Stitch), the legs, antennae, body, and wing markings in black. Fill the wings in with white and the body with yellow. The head is worked in diagonal Cross Stitch.

The blue-green background is worked all around the bee. The front and back part of the seat cover are edged with several rows of Bargello in alternating rows of blue, blue-green, and magenta. The entire background can be worked in Diagonal Tent, and the center can be replaced with another design if desired.

Place the finished canvas on top of the seat cover to check the all-over size, and add a few stitches all around if necessary. Cut out the seat outline, leaving a 1" margin allowance. (Figure 55, A.)

To finish: cut 4" strips diagonally across the 3/4 yard of denim and machine stitch them end to end until they form a strip long enough to go around the seat cover outline. (Figure 55, B.) Fold one edge over about 1" and machine stitch along the fold, leaving a tubular opening of about 3/4".

Fasten the cord or shoe lace to a large safety pin. Slip the closed pin through this tubular opening (Figure 55, C) and pull it through the other end. (Figure 55, D.)

Pin the other edge of the denim strip along the outline of the seat cover wrong sides together. Begin at the back and bring it all around, ending with a slight overlap. Pin into one row of stitches so that the bare canvas threads will not show at the seam. Check the evenness of the outline and correct the pins. Baste all around and remove pins. Finish with two rows of machine stitching and remove basting thread.

Turn the seat cover right-side out (Figure 55, E), slip over the bicycle seat, and pull the cord at both ends. Twist several times around the seat shaft and tie securely. (Figure 56.)

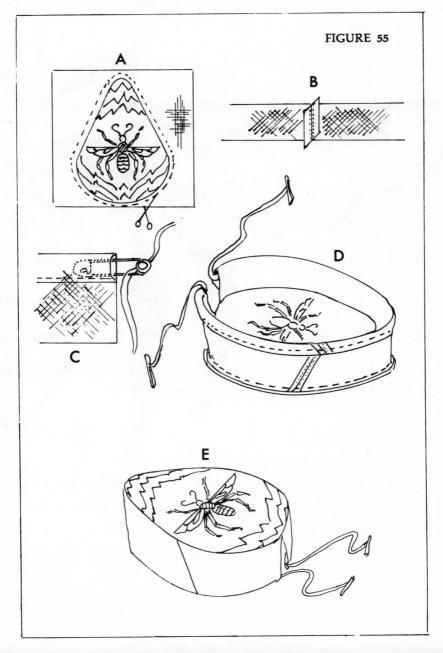

FIGURE 55

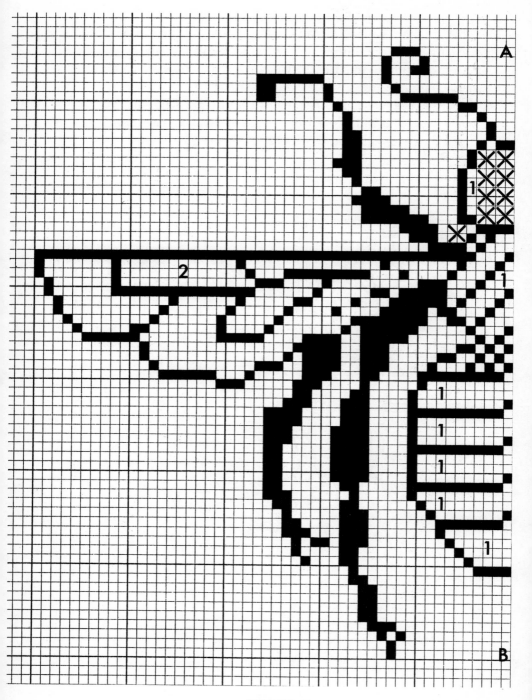

FIGURE 54

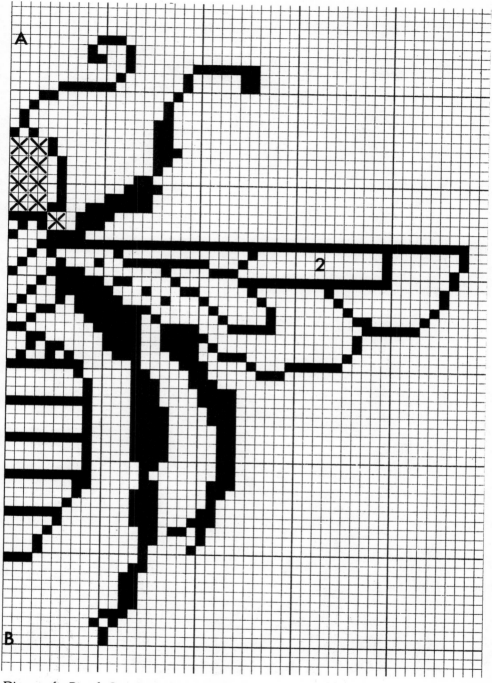

Diagram for Bicycle Seat Cover (see color page):
Black = Black; 1 = Yellow; 2 = White; Background = Pale Green; Bargello
Lines = Shades of Green, Blue-Green, and Magenta.

FIGURE 56

Little Scarecrow Name Plaque

(See color page C2.)

This stylized design can be worked in a number of ways. Here it is worked in a combination of stitches: the jacket is in the Hungarian Stitch pattern; part of the kerchief is in Straight Cross Stitches; the shoes and top of the hat are Diagonal Cross Stitches; the tufts of straw are worked in long random stitches; the hatband, nose, and buttons are in Straight Gobelin; and the rest is in Diagonal Tent (Basketweave).

A child's name is written free-hand in fanciful letters filled with Straight Gobelin on a Basketweave background. The white background is left unworked and bordered with two rows of Straight Stitch Triangles counted out to fit perfectly into a mitered corner.

The entire design may be worked in Basketweave, and the background filled in.

MATERIALS: 18" × 18" square # 12 interlocked mono canvas (includes 2" margin)
Three 8-yard skeins of orange Persian-type yarn, and one skein each of yellow, purple, lavender, brown, light blue, and dark blue
one strand magenta yarn

The black and white photographs (Figures 58 and 59) and the color photograph on color page 2, Bottom, B indicate stitch detail and color placement. The graph outline in Figure 57 can be enlarged according to general enlarging instructions.

Work face in Basketweave, leaving mouth, nose, and eyes unfinished. Place two straight Cross Stitches in blue for eyes, work nose in Straight Gobelin, and make the mouth with one large stitch looped in the center with a small holding stitch and finished at the edges with two diagonal "smile" lines.

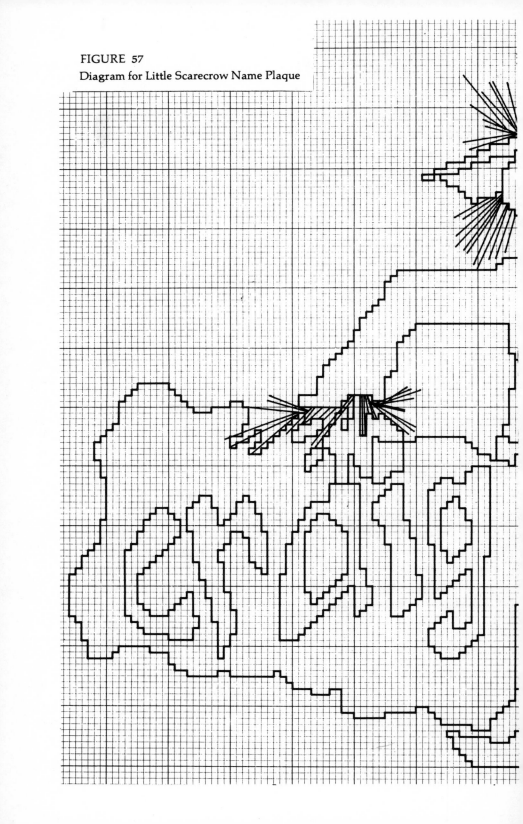

FIGURE 57
Diagram for Little Scarecrow Name Plaque

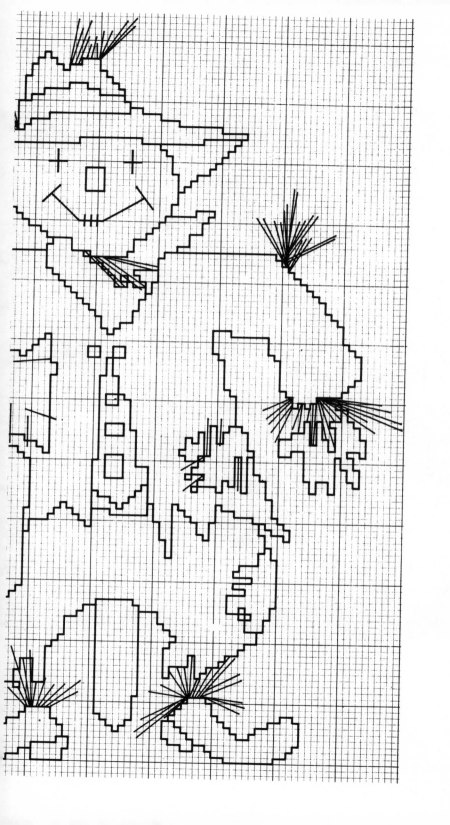

FIGURE 58   Little Scarecrow with Name Plaque (see color page 2, Bottom, B)

FIGURE 59

Enlarged detail for Little Scarecrow with Name Plaque (nose, mouth, and eyes are left unworked, to be over-embroidered after the face background is completed).

Frame for Mirror or Picture

Outline a small mirror in the center of a canvas square and work a variety of stitch patterns in a decorative framework around the outline. (Figure 60.) Stretch the finished work over a flat board. Miter and staple unworked canvas to the back of the board. Then glue a piece of felt over the staples. Glue a bevel-edged mirror or a framed picture in the center of the needlework. Hang with picture wire.

STITCHES: Hungarian Stitch patterns, Straight Gobelin, Smyrna Cross, Scottish Stitch, and Basketweave.

FIGURE 60

Lady With Pickle Jars

(See front cover)

MATERIALS: 17″ × 18″ # 14 interlocked mono canvas (includes a 3″ fold-back margin)

Two 8-yard skeins blue-gray Persian yarn for the dress

Two 8-yard skeins gray Persian yarn for background

Six 8-yard skeins off-white Persian yarn for background

Two 8-yard skeins light brown Persian yarn for floor

1 or 2 strands Persian yarn in assorted colors for jars;

1 strand each in gold, black, and white for kitten

1 strand gold metallic thread for jar caps

The diagram is shown in actual size (11″ × 12″). It is divided into four sections in Figures 61–64. Photocopy or trace each section and assemble at the points indicated by the letters. If the tracing or photocopy is not clearly visible under the canvas, go over the outlines with a medium point marking pen.

Tape the tracing or photocopy to a flat surface and place the canvas over it. Center the design outline carefully and fasten canvas with push pins to prevent it from shifting. Trace design outline with a black acrylic felt-tip pen. There is no need to color the canvas; simply follow the colors indicated in the color photograph on page C3.

The main figure is worked in straight Gobelin in a four-way pattern (Figure 65) with a Smyrna cross in the center. The hair is worked in random long stitches in two or three layers. (See close-up Figure 66.) The arms are worked in straight Gobelin, the cat is worked in fine Kelim stitch in shades of gold, white, and black. The floor is worked in diagonal Parisian long and short stitches in rows from upper right to lower left. The shelves are outlined in chain stitch. The jars are all alike in shape and size and the various contents are suggested by assorted stitches and colors. Follow the numbers for stitches on the diagram outline:

1—Closed herringbone worked sideways

2—Basketweave

3—Basketweave

4—Double cross stitch pattern

5—Double brick stitch
6—Basketweave in two shades of red
7—Straight cross stitch pattern
8—Rococo stitch pattern

The jar caps are worked with long horizontal lines in yellow yarn alternating with gold metallic thread. The background is worked in off-white and gray.

FIGURE 65

Enlarged stitch detail for
dress of Lady with Pickle Jars.

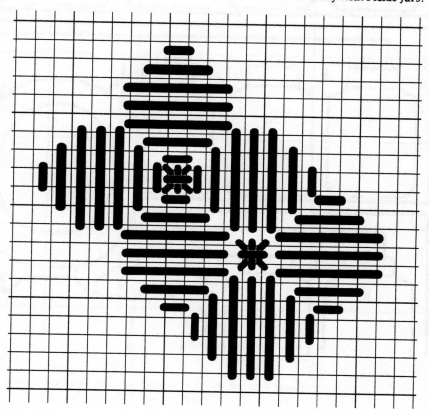

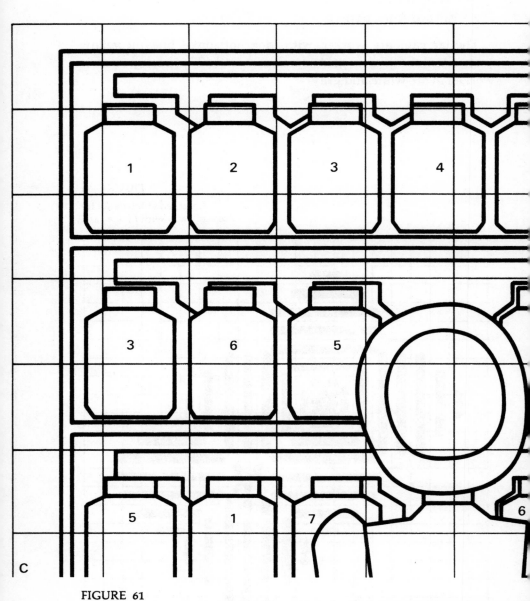

C

FIGURE 61

Actual-size diagram for Lady with Pickle Jars (see front cover).
Trace and align A–A, B–B, C–C, D–D, E–E for full pattern.

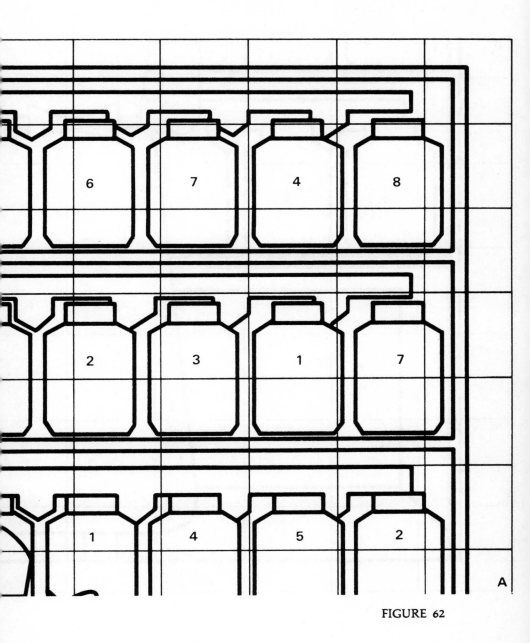

FIGURE 62

C

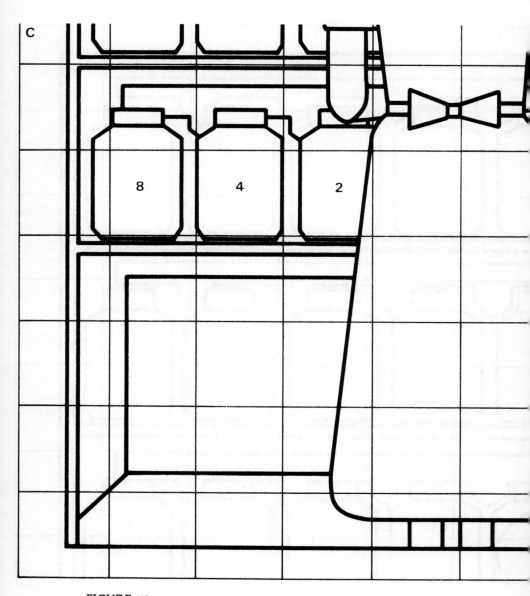

FIGURE 63

94

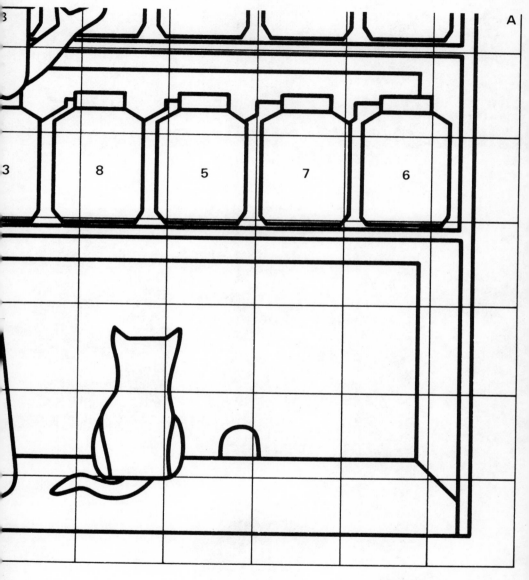

3

3

8

5

7

6

A

FIGURE 64

95

A Word about Commercial Kits

Commercial kits were once considered a waste of time and talent. More often than not this criticism was well-founded because kits were for the most part a catch-all of bad designs, discontinued yarn colors, and inaccurate stenciling methods.

Today, packaged needlepoint kits have come a long way. To meet the standards of an ever-increasing number of sophisticated needleworkers, manufacturers have replaced the shabby materials with a new line of fresh, attractive designs.

A large number of companies produce and package a variety of kits for anything from pin cushions to rugs, as well as prefabricated articles such as belts, tennis racquet covers, vests, and handbags.

A good shop will be selective in its choice of stock. It will also carry a line of painted needlepoint canvases and assist you in selecting the right yarns. A beginner may find a kit more relaxing as a first project.

You can personalize a commercial kit by changing some or all of the colors and by introducing different stitch patterns within the design or the background.

FIGURE 66

SINGLE STITCHES
AND
STITCH PATTERNS

This chapter presents all of the stitches (besides the combination stitches) which are used in the projects.

FIGURE 67. Running Stitch

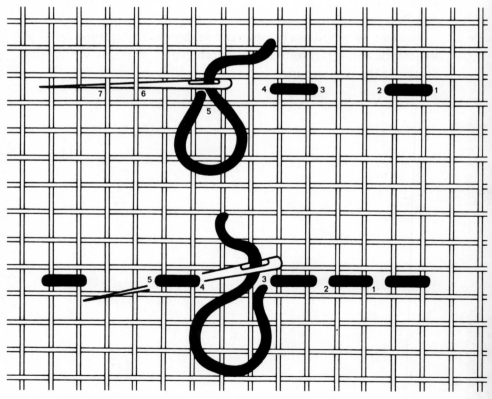

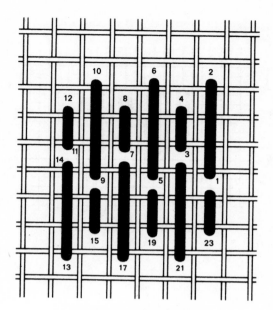

FIGURE 68. Parisian Stitch

FIGURE 69. Straight Gobelin

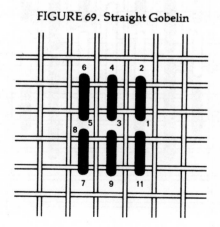

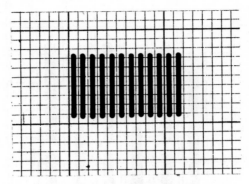

FIGURE 70. Satin Stitch

FIGURE 71. Hungarian Stitch pattern

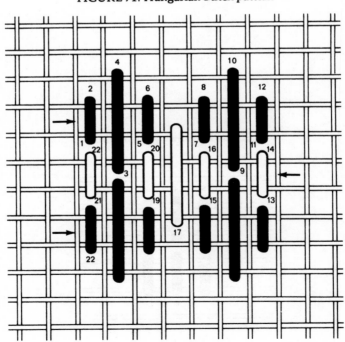

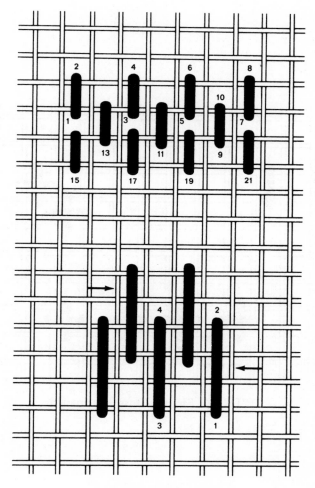

FIGURE 72. Brick Stitch

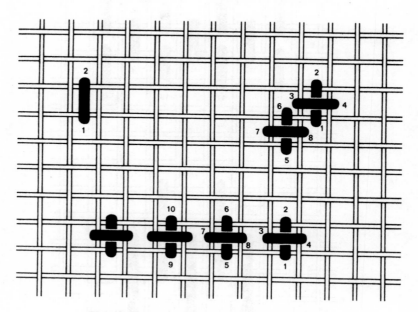

FIGURE 73. Straight Cross Stitch pattern

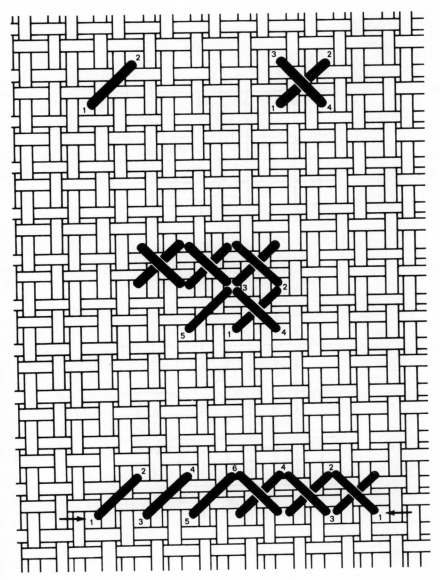

FIGURE 74. Diagonal Cross Stitch pattern

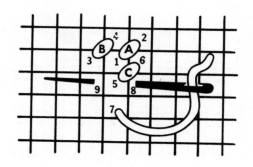

FIGURE 75. Basketweave

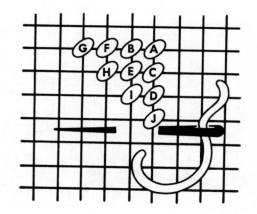

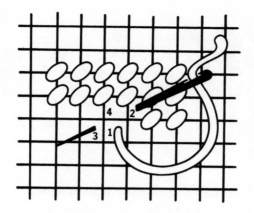

FIGURE 76. Continental Stitch

FIGURE 77. Scottish Stitch pattern

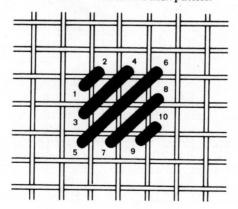

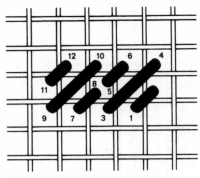

FIGURE 78. Mosaic Stitch pattern

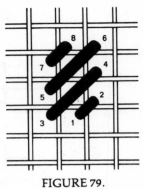

FIGURE 79.
Cashmere Stitch pattern

FIGURE 80. Buttonhole, or Blanket Stitch

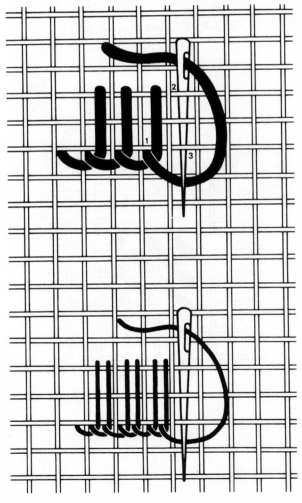

106

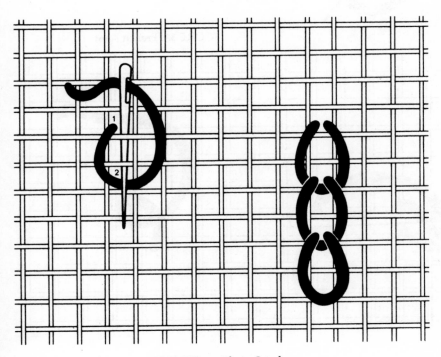

FIGURE 81. Chain Stitch

FIGURE 82. Feather Stitch

FIGURE 83. French Knot

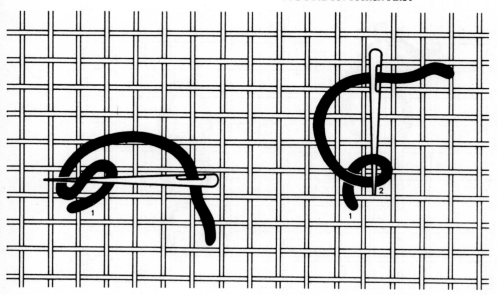

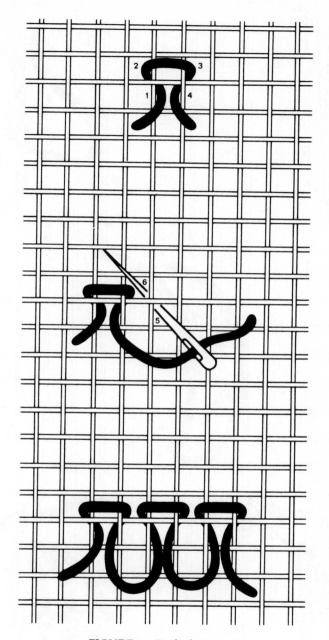

FIGURE 84. Turkish Knot

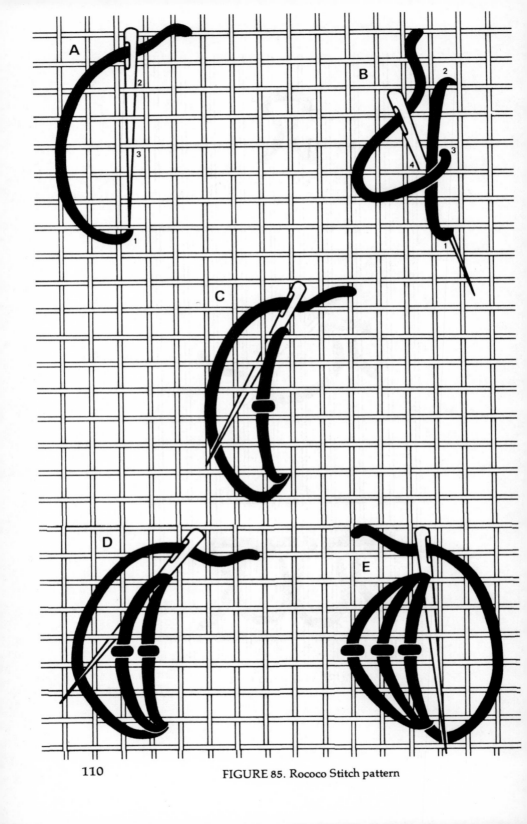

FIGURE 85. Rococo Stitch pattern

FINISHING AND MOUNTING NEEDLEWORK

Blocking Needlework

Blocking is the method by which needlework is straightened and stitches evened. Blocking is a finishing process and always necessary unless the needlework was stitched on a frame.

Crewel and Bargello stitchery fluff out beautifully with blocking, and a good blocking can do wonders for any distorted canvas.

The best blocking surface is composition board. This is a specially processed material available in lumber yards. It does not warp, and it accommodates nails without splitting or throwing off splinters.

Buy a composition board that is a few inches larger than the largest work you are likely to block. For any project larger than 30" × 30", I recommend professional blocking.

You will also need a box of heavy-duty inch-long nails with large heads, a good heavy hammer, a thick terry towel, an iron, a pencil, and a ruler.

With pencil and ruler, outline the original outer dimensions of the entire canvas. Draw lines right on the board, and place the work to be blocked within this outline. Of the four corners in the canvas, two will be very pointed (Figure 86, BB) and the other two rather shallow (Figure 86, AA). The last two (opposite corners) should be nailed first. Fasten one into the outlined corner with two or three nails; pull the other one in the opposite direction and nail it into that corner. (Figure 87.) These two corners will offer the most resistance to blocking, so be sure to fasten them securely with several nails. Now pull the lateral sides of the canvas and nail them along the penciled outline. Drive nails halfway into the board about 1" apart.

FIGURE 86

Blunt-nosed pliers are helpful in stretching canvas, and nails should be driven into the unfinished margins only.

A distorted canvas should be blocked face-up so that the stitches can be watched as they are being stretched into shape. The crucial test is the stretch point between the *A* corners in Figure 87. The better it squares off, the more even the needlework will be.

FIGURE 87

When blocking is completed, place a damp (not wet) terry towel over the canvas and glide a hot iron over it until it stops steaming. Repeat this several times. Let dry at least twenty-four hours, and then steam again. Remove nails after two or three days, and let the canvas rest a day or two. If some of the distortion reappears, there is little you can do. No additional blocking will restore the canvas.

Framing or upholstering will preserve the design, but a soft hanging or a pillow will have to be adjusted by cutting away the distorted corners.

Note: It is not necessary to soak canvas needlework before blocking. Soaking makes the work slippery; and if too much sizing penetrates the yarn, the stitches will stiffen as they dry. If canvas resists stretching, mist it slightly to relax the threads. Use a misting device designed for spraying house plants. Raised or textured stitches should not be pressed at all. Mist the canvas on the reverse side, and block it right-side up.

Blocking Textured Needlework

Textured stitches worked on soft fabrics have a tendency to pucker the fabric and make it appear wrinkled. A large work is normally done on a frame, in which case it needs little or no blocking.

Any embroidery worked in the hand needs to be blocked, however. You will need a flat smooth board, such as an old oak table-top or a piece of composition board. Do not use plywood, veneered wood, or any warped surface. The board should be somewhat larger than the needlework.

Wet the fabric lightly with a spray mist of water. Mist the wrong side and turn it over to block right-side up. Stretch and pull the fabric gently but firmly, placing push pins all around the worked area. The fabric should be smooth and wrinkle-free and the weave of the threads very straight. As the fabric is stretched, the stitches will lift and fluff out. Let the piece dry at room temperature, and then remove it from the board. This method is more satisfactory than steam ironing, which tends to pucker the fabric around the heavier stitches.

Mitering Fabric

Mitering produces neat corners when folding square or rectangular fabrics. To miter fabric, draw the desired outline on the blocked or pressed fabric. Cut loose threads and frayed edges and leave an even border all around. (Figure 88, A.) Clip and fold the corners as indicated in Figure 88, B. Fold sides evenly as shown in Figure 88, C. Pin folds in place. Stitch all around, remove pins, and press.

When lining rugs or wall hangings that are too bulky to stitch and turn inside out, miter the needlework and the lining separately, and stitch back-to-back.

Note: Make the lining somewhat smaller, and on wall hangings leave the bottom edges open.

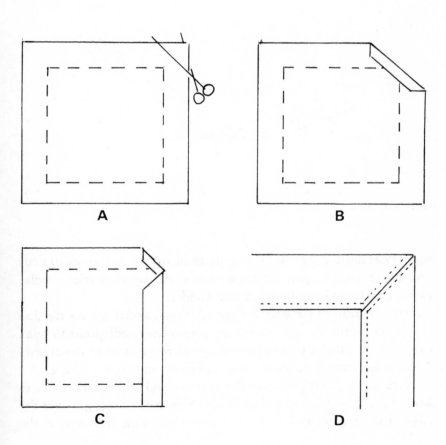

A

B

C

D

Framing Needlework

A needlework canvas cannot be framed like a photograph or poster, nor should it be glued to a board. For best results it must be stretched on a frame.

The best frame for needlework is the simple, sturdy artist's frame. These frames are sold in individual strips of 6" and up. Each end of the strip is grooved and mitered for easy assembly.

After a needlework has been stretched on an artist's frame, it can be slipped into a decorative frame. These frames are sold in packages of pre-finished strips of one length. Since frame sizes are

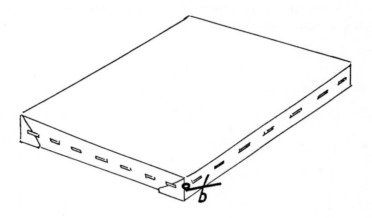

somewhat limited, check the supply of ready-made frames in your area before deciding on the design and dimensions of your needlework, otherwise have them custom-made.

Once the frames have been selected, finish and block the needlepoint. Assemble the artist's frame, steam the needlepoint to relax canvas (see blocking information), and place it over the frame. The worked area should not extend over the edge of the frame.

Place a few push pins into the corners and around the sides to keep the canvas from shifting. Fold the unworked margin over the edge of the frame, and staple the center point on each side of the frame. The rows of stitches should look straight and the needle-work smooth and even. Be careful not to overstretch.

Staple all around the frame, folding the corners neatly as shown in Figure 89. If the staples protrude slightly, hammer them in. If a professional stapler is not available, use carpet tacks placed 1/4" apart.

Cut the canvas along the edges, and place the finished piece in a decorative frame. Do not place glass over needlework unless you are framing a fragile antique; and in that case, have a professional do the job. Antique frames can be used for needlework if they are deep enough to accommodate the artist's frame. A frame that was used for an oil painting is more suitable than one used for a photograph. Custom frames should always be handled by a professional.

Note: The edge of the decorative frame should cover one or two rows of stitched canvas all around. Allow for this in the preliminary planning of the needlepoint.

How to Make a Pillow

The loveliest pillows are usually the simplest to make. They show off the stitchery with a minimum of frills and ruffles.

MATERIALS: Fabric backing in the same size and approximate weight as the needlework (velvet, duck, upholstery fabric, etc.)
Pillow filler, 1" larger than needlework (choose dacron polyester or feathers and down—both are available ready-made in department stores
Decorative twisted cord or braid (optional)

Press fabric and pin to blocked needlework with right sides together. Stitch several rows of large basting (running) stitches across the entire width of the two fabrics at 2" intervals. These basting stitches will keep both fabrics flat and even.

Remove pins, and machine stitch on the needlepoint side as indicated in Figure 90. Two rows of machine stitches sewn at the widest setting are better than one row of little stitches.

Clip corners at points and cut seams to 1/4", then remove basting threads. Turn pillow right-side out. Poke out the corners with your fingers.

Measure the entire outline of the pillow, and cut a length of cord or braid one inch longer. Don't stretch the cord while measuring. Tie a piece of thread close to the cut edges to prevent the cord from separating.

Beginning at the open end, pin the cord along the edge of the pillow to cover the machine stitching. Take small stitches in matching thread and stop at the other end of the pillow opening. Secure the cord at that point with an extra stitch, and remove the needle. Finish stitching the cord after the pillow is stuffed.

To stuff pillow, push a cotton ball into each corner, then insert the pillow filler. Fold the filler in half, slip it into the opening, and unfold it inside the casing. Handstitch the opening closed by folding the needlework and fabric backing into the opening and lining up the edge with the existing machine stitching.

Re-thread the needle on the decorative cord, and stitch it over the closed edge. Overlap the end pieces of the cord and tie the remaining thread over the two to keep them from unravelling. End with a few stitches.

Note: The opening and the ends of the decorative cord should be placed at the bottom line of the pillow. Check the needlepoint design before basting the outline.

LIST OF SUPPLIERS

Retail Only

La Stitcherie
72 Middle Neck Road
Great Neck, New York 11021

Canvas, yarn, kits, custom designs

Wholesale and Retail

Toni Toes of Vermont, Inc.
Route 100
South Londonderry, Vermont 05155

Handbags, kits for tennis racquet covers, belts for needlepoint, plastic enclosures
Will send catalogue

Walbead, Inc.
38 West 37th Street
New York, New York 10018

Beads, sequins, macrame
Will send catalogue

Wholesale Only

Paternayan Brothers, Inc.
312 East 95th Street
New York, New York 10028

Paternayan Persian yarn, canvas and needles, rug and crewel yarns, Rya cloth

Craft Yarns of Rhode Island
P.O. Box 151
Harrisville, R.I.

Three-ply Persian-type yarn, quick-point yarn, needlepoint canvas

Coats and Clark's
P.O. Box 1966
Stamford, Connecticut 06904

Cotton and rayon embroidery threads and rug yarns, craft yarns (acrylic washable), acrylic Persian-type yarn, needles

Handwork Tapestries
114 B Allen Blvd.
Farmingdale, New York 11735

Persian-type yarn, Laine Colbert three-ply tapestry yarn, Colbert six, French silk, canvas

Art Needlework Treasure Trove
P.O. Box 2440
Grand Central Station
New York, New York 10017

Canvas, yarns, linens, embroidery fabrics, and supplies

Howard Needlework Supply Co., Inc. 919 Third Avenue New York, New York 10022	Canvas and embroidery fabric in linen, cotton, and polyester
William E. Wright Co. One Penn Plaza New York, New York 10001	Lace
E.T. Group Ltd. 230 Fifth Avenue New York, New York 10017	Paternayan yarns, Alice Peterson painted canvases, Rya cloth
George Wells The Ruggery Cedar Swamp Road Glen Head, New York 11545	Rug yarns, linen and Rya cloth, undyed yarn, special dyes for wool yarns, Hectograph pencils
Astor Place Ltd. 260 Main Avenue Stirling, New Jersey 07980	Painted canvases and packaged kits
Cute and Custom 1A Munson Court Melville, New York 11746	Painted canvases and packaged kits
Needlepoint U.S.A. 37 West 57th Street New York, New York 10019	Painted canvases and packaged kits

Note: For all inquiries to dealers, enclose a self-addressed stamped envelope.